Presented to:

_____

From:

_____

Published in Nashville, Tennessee, by Thomas Nelson. Thomas Nelson is a
trademark of Thomas Nelson, Inc.

Published in association with Yates & Yates (www.yates2.com)

Content Editors: Cathy Lord and Beau Sager

Project Editor: Lisa Stilwell

Page Designer: Walter Petrie

Thomas Nelson, Inc., titles may be purchased in bulk for educational,
business, fund-raising, or sales promotional use. For information, please
e-mail SpecialMarkets@ThomasNelson.com.

Unless otherwise stated, Scripture references are taken from the NEW KING
JAMES VERSION. © 1982, 1992, by Thomas Nelson, Inc. Used by
permission. All rights reserved.

Other Scripture is taken from HOLY BIBLE: NEW INTERNATIONAL
VERSION® (NIV). © 1973, 1978, 1984 by International Bible Society.
Used by permission of Zondervan Publishing House. All rights reserved. *Holy
Bible*, New Living Translation (NLT) © 1996. Used by permission of
Tyndale House Publishers, Inc., Wheaton, Ill. All rights reserved. KING
JAMES VERSION (KJV).

ISBN 978-1-4041-8781-8

Printed in the United States of America

10 11 12 13 14 LBM 5 4 3

The
Prophecy
ANSWER
BOOK

DAVID JEREMIAH

THOMAS NELSON
Since 1798

NASHVILLE   DALLAS   MEXICO CITY   RIO DE JANEIRO

Table of Contents

Introduction

Any study of the End Times can create a variety of questions, concerns, and even confusion in our minds. Sometimes it is difficult to see how obscure passages, distant places, and unfamiliar symbols can have any significance for our lives. After all, if we can't understand what the Bible is teaching, how in the world can it have any relevance to what we are experiencing today?

I don't want you to miss the rich truth God has provided for us in the Bible.

To help you understand and appreciate this topic, I have compiled a list of questions and answers to the most frequently asked questions about biblical prophecy. I hope these answers about current events, the Rapture, the Tribulation, the Second Coming, and the new heaven and the new earth will help you live with confidence and hope in a time that is filled with all kinds of uncertainty and trouble.

We must remember that prophecy is important to God and He desires us to understand His plan for the future. There are more than nine hundred prophecies in the Bible concerning the second coming of Jesus Christ—nearly three times as many compared to His first coming! In the Bible, God has taken great care to communicate this to us in a way we can understand.

Jesus tells us to keep our eyes open so we are not fooled by the signs indicating that the End Times are near. As we get closer to the End Times, many people are going to claim to be the Messiah and claim to have the answers for a troubled world. Additionally, the book of Revelation tells us to expect a period of ceaseless, unending, terrible war. It appears that we are already preparing for this time as fifty percent of all research scientists today are involved in arms development and there is at least one military weapon and four thousand pounds of explosives for every man, woman, and child on earth. Finally, there will be more and more disease and devastation. Today, as you read this, millions of people in the world are being afflicted by insufficient food, the spread of new diseases, and the devastating effects of natural disasters. As we get closer to the End Times, there will be more and more famine. There will also be an increase in earthquakes and natural disasters. Christ also spoke of pestilence: the spread of new diseases. Our world will experience a spate of tragic new diseases that we will be unable to control.

Seeing these signs played out in the newspaper and on television, over the Internet and even in our own lives, can cause despair, anxiety, and confusion. When Jesus tells us to open our eyes, He does so in order to encourage us to gaze upon Him—not because this will cause all of the world's problems (and ours) to disappear but because He is the Prince of Peace. In the pages that follow, I encourage you to study God's plan for the future with me as I open the Scriptures. I am confident you will find, as I have, that studying and understanding the events of tomorrow will help you live with confidence and hope today.

— Awaiting His return,
David Jeremiah

Current Events

THE BIBLE HAS PROVEN TO BE ABSOLUTELY DEPENDABLE. THEREFORE WE CAN TRUST IT AS THE SOURCE OF RELIABLE INFORMATION ABOUT THE MEANING OF THE EVENTS OF OUR DAY AND WHAT THOSE EVENTS TELL US ABOUT OUR HOPE FOR THE FUTURE AS WE LOOK TOWARD THE RETURN OF CHRIST. THE LORD JESUS HIMSELF SPOKE OF THE WISDOM OF DISCERNING THE SIGNS OF THE TIMES AND OF TAKING APPROPRIATE ACTION AS WE WAIT FOR HIS RETURN (MATTHEW 24, MARK 13).

Now as He sat on the Mount of Olives, the disciples came to Him privately, saying, "Tell us, when will these things be? And what will be the sign of Your coming, and of the end of the age?"

Matthew 24:3

Why is a fledgling country [Israel] with a population of slightly more than seven million and a total land space hardly larger than New Jersey mentioned in the nightly news more than any other nation except the United States and why is Israel important in prophecy?

For answers we must turn not to the evening news or the front page of the newspaper, but to the Bible.

Israel's story begins with God's sovereign purpose revealed in the first book of the Bible, Genesis. Apparently God finds Abraham and his descendants to be of enormous importance. The very proportion of the coverage tells us something about the importance of Israel. Only two chapters are given to the whole story of creation.

One chapter records the fall of man. Eight chapters cover the thousands of years from creation to the time of Abraham. Then we find that fully thirty-eight chapters deal with the life stories of Abraham, Isaac, and Jacob—the progenitors of the Jewish race.

Israel is important because the fulfillment of God's covenant with its founder Abraham greatly affects every one of us. The playing out of prophetic events concerning Israel places us in the last days of history's timeline. The miraculous survival of God's covenant people, the Jews, demonstrates God's providence and His ability to accomplish His purpose in the face of what seems to human minds impossible odds. The existence of Israel today is exhibit A in the lineup of convincing evidences that the Bible's prophecies concerning the future will be fulfilled. To this day, the issue of who controls Israel, the Promised Land, is the most volatile in international politics.

Do the boundaries of present-day Israel fulfill God's promise to Israel in the Old Testament?

The land promised to Abraham covers much more area than what the present nation of Israel occupies. Genesis 15:18 tells us that it stretches all the way from the Mediterranean Sea on the west to the Euphrates River on the east. Ezekiel fixes the northern boundary of Israel at Hamath, one hundred miles north of Damascus (Ezekiel 48:1), and the southern boundary at Kadesh, about one hundred miles south of Jerusalem (v. 48:28).

BOUNDARIES OF GOD'S COVENANT LAND

Today, Israel is one-nineteenth the size of California and roughly the size of our third smallest state, New Jersey. It is 260 miles at its longest point, 60 miles at its widest, and three miles at its narrowest.

When you look at a map and locate that tiny strip of land that Israel now claims, you can see that she does not now, nor has she ever, fully occupied the land that was described to Abraham in God's covenant promise. If Israel were currently occupying all the land promised to her, she would control present-day Israel, Lebanon, the West Bank of Jordan, and substantial portions of Syria, Iraq, and Saudi Arabia.

> Will the Jews ever realize the fulfillment of God's covenant to possess Israel as an everlasting possession?

The prophet Isaiah asserted that it would happen. He prophesied that the Lord would "set His hand again the second time to recover the remnant of His people who are left" (Isaiah 11:11). God also addressed the issue through Ezekiel when He said, "I will take you from among the nations, gather you out of all countries, and bring you into your own land" (Ezekiel 36:24).

The fulfillment of those prophecies was set in motion on May 14, 1948, when the U.S. recognized the new state of Israel. On the evening of that announcement, popular radio commentator Lowell Thomas said in his broadcast that Americans in every part of the country would be turning to their Bibles for historical background enabling them to understand "this day in history."[1] And indeed, as prophecies found in Isaiah, Ezekiel, Matthew, and Revelation show, both the Old

Testament and the New Testament pointed to this day when the Jews would return to the land promised them and initiate fulfillment of the ancient prophecies.

The Israeli government established the State of Israel, thus fulfilling the twenty-five-hundred-year-old prophecy recorded in the Bible.

> Is Israel's presence in her land today the final fulfillment of God's promise to regather His people?

The answer is no! What is happening in Israel today is primarily the result of a secular Zionist movement, whereas Ezekiel wrote about a spiritual return of God's people to Him when he said:

> For I will take you from the nations, gather you from all the lands and bring you into your own land . . . . Moreover, I will give you a new heart and put a new spirit within you; . . . I will put My Spirit within you and cause you to walk in My statutes, and you will be careful to observe My ordinances. You will live in the land that I gave to your forefathers; so you will be My people, and I will be your God (Ezekiel 36:24–28 NASB).

The return of Jews to the newly refounded nation of Israel is the first stage of that regathering, but it certainly does not fulfill the requirements of a spiritual return to the Lord.

> From the moment of God's promise to Abraham to this present hour, the prophecies concerning Israel's total possession and blessing in the land remain unfulfilled. The most dramatic events lie ahead of us.

I srael has been attacked over and over since its founding, sometimes in all-out wars and incessantly by
terrorists. The Jewish people have survived by remaining
vigilant, but they long for peace. According to the Bible,
a future leader will fulfill this longing by brokering a
seven-year peace deal with Israel's enemies. But Scripture
also tells us that this peace plan will be broken, and Israel
will be attacked once again, this time as never before.
Countless armies will amass against the boxed-in nation,
leaving it with no human hope of victory. Only Christ's
return, His judgment, and His reign will finally bring
true peace to Israel.

It is then that God's covenant with Abraham will
reach its ultimate fulfillment. The Jews will return to
the Lord and, as Ezekiel and Jeremiah prophesied, they
will be His people and He will be their God. The bor-
ders of the land will expand to the dimensions described
in Genesis 15 and Ezekiel 48. Christ's return will also

fulfill the prophecy of Jeremiah that God would gather the Jews: "Behold, I will gather them out of all countries where I have driven them . . . I will bring them back to this place, and I will cause them to dwell safely. They shall be My people, and I will be their God" (Jeremiah 32:37–38).

Ezekiel makes it clear that this gathering means God will return every single living Jew back to their land. For he writes that the Lord said He would gather them again to their own land "and . . . none of them [will be] captive any longer" (Ezekiel 39:28).

Today we see this prophecy being fulfilled right before our eyes. In 2006, for the first time in nineteen hundred years, Israel became home to the largest Jewish community in the world, surpassing the Jewish population in the United States. From the 650,000 who returned when the Jewish state was founded in 1948, the population of Israel has swelled to approximately 5.4 million, and it is expected to exceed 6 million by 2020.[2]

Does oil hold a key to the prophetic events of the future?

Oil explains why the Bible focuses its end-time attention on the Middle East, and, more than any factor other than the nation of Israel oil, holds the key to the prophetic events of the future.

Few would question the fact that oil has become the new basis for our world economy. It is now the stuff of life, the commodity most highly valued by the industrialized and emerging nations of the world, the blood that flows through their economic veins and gives life to prosperity in today's global economy. The greatest source of that lifeblood is now in the Middle East, and so that is where the eyes of the world are focused.

What does this tell us about coming events? In Luke's gospel, Jesus contrasts our ability to discern weather signs with our inability to understand the more important signs of the time: "You can discern the face of the sky and of the earth, but how is it that you do not discern this time?" (Luke 12:56). Surely the world's fascination with oil—a highly valuable commodity with a source in lands hostile or borderline hostile to Israel and to us—qualifies as a "sign."

What do oil and the garden of Eden have in common?

My friend Robert Morgan flew into New Orleans several years ago, and the man who met him at the airport was a geophysicist for a major oil company. Driving to the hotel, he explained to Robert that oil deposits result from the decomposition of plant and animal life now buried by eons of time. Oil is found all over the world, he said, even under the ice of the Arctic and Antarctic. That means forests and abundant vegetation once covered the world until destroyed in a vast global cataclysm (such as a worldwide flood).

The geophysicist went on to say that the earth's richest, deepest, and largest deposits of petroleum lie under the sands of countries just to the east of Israel in the location pinpointed in the Bible as the garden of Eden. Eden was a teeming expanse of forests, foliage, and gardens with rich fertility unparalleled in human history.

Barren sand and blazing desert now exist where once grew a garden flourishing with dense, lush flora, the likes of which the world has not seen since. It was destroyed in some disastrous upheaval and has decayed into the largest deposits of oil in the world. I had never before imagined that the gasoline I pump into my car might be the ruined remains of the rich, vast foliage of the garden of Eden.

It's ironic to think that Satan may finance the Battle of Armageddon at the end of human history with revenues generated from the garden he spoiled at the beginning of human history.[3]

Oil explains why the Bible focuses its end-time attention on the Middle East.

How does today's oil situation align with prophecy?

Since there are no substantive oil deposits in Israel today, we must continue to deal with the reality of a world in which oil remains in the possession of countries hostile to us and to Israel. For example, Ezekiel foretold a time when Russia would attack Israel. In detailing how the military aggression would take place, the prophet listed a coalition of some of the nations that would join with Russia in the attack. "Persia, Ethiopia, and Libya are with them, all of them with shield and helmet" (Ezekiel 38:5).

Until March 21, 1935, Persia was the official name of the country we now call Iran. Not once in the past twenty-five hundred years has Russia formed a military connection with Persia/Iran—until now.[4] But now these two nations have formed a military alliance that continues to be strengthened by the political situation in our world. Russia recently signed a billion-dollar deal to sell missiles and other weaponry to Iran. And the connection is even broader, as Joel C. Rosenberg, former aide to Israeli Prime Minister Benjamin Netanyahu, points out:

"Over 1000 Iranian nuclear scientists have been trained in Russia by senior Russian scientists."[5] Here is an end-time alliance that was prophesied twenty-five hundred years ago, and in the last few years it has become a reality. Obviously, the stage is being set!

Oil is the new gold in the world economy and holds the key to the prophetic events of the future.

What is America's place in end-time prophecy?

No specific mention of the United States or any other country in North or South America can be found in the Bible. One reason may be that in the grand scheme of history, the U.S. is a new kid on the block. As a nation, it is less than 250 years old—much younger than the nations of Bible times that are featured in biblical prophecy. In fact, the Bible makes no mention of most nations in the modern world. The ancient prophets were primarily concerned with the Holy Land and its immediate neighbors. Areas remote from Israel do not figure in prophecy and are not mentioned in the Bible.

John Walvoord posited one theory that suggests, "America will be in the mix of the political realignments that foreshadow the end of time through our nations of origin. Most citizens of the United States of America have come from Europe, and their sympathies would more naturally be with a European alliance. . . ."[6] And we can see signs of such realignments taking place today.

With the usual presidential fanfare in April of

2007, President Bush welcomed European Union Commission President Jos Barroso and the serving President of the European Council, German Chancellor Angela Merkel, in the Rose Garden of the White House. These three leaders signed the Framework for Advancing Transatlantic Economic Integration between the United States of America and the European Union. Less than seven months after its signing, the Transatlantic Economic Council held its first official meeting in Washington, D.C. In a joint statement it was announced, "Since April, the United States and the European Union have made substantial progress in removing barriers to trade and investment and in easing regulatory burdens."[7]

On the surface there seems to be nothing ominous about such an agreement; it appears to be simply about freeing up economic trade between nations. But a similar, less publicized meeting was held in March 2008 at the State Department, which focused on linking the U.S., Mexico, and Canada in a "North American community with the European Union" in anticipation of the "creation of a 'Transatlantic Economic Union' between the European Union and North America." One participant—whose identity is protected by the Chatham House Rule, which permits information to be disseminated without attribution to guarantee confidentiality—made this revealing statement:

> North America should be a premiere platform to establish continental institutions. That's why we need to move the security perimeters to include the whole continent, especially as we open the borders between North American countries for expanding free trade.[8]

Statements such as this reveal an intention toward union that has implications far beyond mere economic trade. And considering the speed at which leaders are pushing union between nations, it appears that it will not be long before we see such a union instituted.

Is the unification of Europe foretold in Scripture?

M ore than two thousand years ago, God gave His servant Daniel a vision of the future that we recognize as the most comprehensive prophetic insight ever given to man. Through Daniel, God gave a composite history of the remaining days of the world. The first kingdom was Babylon, which was to be followed by the Medes and Persians, the Greeks, the Romans, and the last world kingdom which would be made up from a restored Roman Empire.

According to Daniel, there is to be yet another division of the Roman Empire. He foretells a time when the Roman Empire will consist of ten kingdoms or leaders (Daniel 2:41–43; 7:7, 24). We know this ten-kingdom prophecy remains in the future because not only has the ten-leader form of the Roman Empire never existed in history, but neither has such a kingdom been suddenly crushed as prophecy indicates. Daniel 2 states that the Roman Empire in its final form will experience sudden destruction. The Roman Empire of Jesus' day did not end suddenly. It gradually deteriorated and declined over many centuries until the western part, the Holy Roman Empire, fell in AD 476, and the eastern part, the Byzantine Empire, fell in AD 1453. You can hardly imagine a more gradual slide from glory to oblivion! We must conclude, then, that some form of the Roman Empire must emerge in the end times, and according to Daniel, it will be in place prior to the coming of Christ to rule and reign over the earth. The unification of Europe is really the reunification of the Roman Empire. Today the concentration of power in the European Union signals the beginning of a new world order.

Will there be a one world leader?

According to Daniel's prophecy, a supreme leader will rise from among the ten-leader confederacy in Europe: "And another shall rise after them; he shall be different from the first ones, and shall subdue three kings. He shall speak pompous words against the Most High, shall persecute the saints of the Most High, and shall intend to change times and law. Then the saints shall be given into his hand for a time and times and half a time" (Daniel 7:24–25). This leader will become the final world dictator. We know him as the Antichrist. The new European Union is one of the conditional preludes to the coming of the Antichrist. As Arno Froese, executive director of Midnight Call Ministries, writes:

> The new European power structure will fulfill the prophetic predictions which tell us that a one world system will be implemented. When established, it will fall into the hands of the Antichrist.[9]

Will there be a treaty between
the one world leader and
Israel?

I n the ninth chapter of Daniel's prophecy, he tells us
of a treaty that will be signed between God's people
and the world leader who will head the realigned Roman
Empire: "Then he shall confirm a covenant with many
for one week, but in the middle of the week he shall
bring an end to sacrifice and offering" (Daniel 9:27).
Daniel tells us here that Israel will sign a treaty with the
Antichrist, and that this treaty will be forged to last for
a "week," literally in prophetic language, a "week of
years," or seven years. This treaty will be an attempt to
settle the Arab-Israeli controversy that today focuses the
world's attention on the Middle East. After three and
one-half years, that treaty will be broken, and the count-
down to Armageddon will begin.

The prophecies of Daniel show us what time it is: the hands on the prophetic clock are moving toward midnight. The warning has been sounded, and we will do well to heed it.

What is the Axis of Evil?

On January 29, 2002, in his State of the Union address, President George W. Bush used the term *Axis of Evil* for the first time. He identified Iran, Iraq, and North Korea as "states . . . [who are] arming to threaten the peace of the world . . . These regimes," he said, "pose a grave threat and growing danger. They could provide these arms to terrorists, giving them the means to match their hatred."[10] On May 6, 2002, U.S. Ambassador to the United Nations John Bolton gave a speech titled, "Beyond the Axis of Evil" in which he added three more rogue states to the axis: Libya, Syria, and Cuba. Today the term *Axis of Evil* includes all six states.

Why is one particular nation
that is on the Axis of Evil list
of special interest to us?

One nation on this Axis of Evil list is of special interest to us because we find that it is also on God's list. That nation, Iran, and that list are found in the 38th and 39th chapters of Ezekiel. These chapters, written some twenty-six hundred years ago, give us one of the most important and dramatic prophecies in all Scripture. It is commonly referred to as the prophecy against Gog and Magog, and it is the most detailed prophecy concerning war in the entire Bible. The prophecy predicts an invasion of Israel in the last days— an invasion comprised of enormous masses of troops from a coalition of nations led by Iran and Russia.

This invasion will occur shortly after Israel signs a covenant with the new leader of the European Union. Because of this agreement, Israel will be at peace with her Islamic neighbors. The people of Israel will believe that the European powers will protect them from any outside aggressor or invader . . . especially from Russia, which will have joined forces with Iran to develop weapons for the purpose of utterly destroying Israel.

The events unfolding in today's world are ominously threatening to unsettle institutions, reorder national political alignments, change the balance of world power, and destabilize the equitable distribution of resources.

What present-day nations will form a coalition that will march against Israel as prophesied by Ezekiel?

Now the word of the LORD came to me, saying, "Son of man, set your face against Gog, of the land of Magog, the prince of Rosh, Meshech, and Tubal, and prophesy against him, and say, 'Thus says the Lord GOD: "Behold, I am against you, O Gog, the prince of Rosh, Meshech, and Tubal. I will turn you around, put hooks into your jaws, and lead you out, with all your army, horses, and horsemen, all splendidly clothed, a great company with bucklers and shields, all of them handling swords. Persia, Ethiopia, and Libya are with them, all of them with shield and helmet; Gomer and all its troops; the house of Togarmah from the far north and all its troops—many people are with you. Prepare yourself and be ready, you and all your companies that are gathered about you; and be a guard for them'" (Ezekiel 38:1–7).

As you can see, Ezekiel's prophecy begins with a list of proper names. Many of these names identify certain grandchildren and great-grandchildren of Noah who were the fathers of nations that for a time bore their names (see Genesis 10). These nations, which today no longer bear their original names, will ultimately form a coalition that will march against Israel. As we identify these nations by their present names and locate them on today's world map, we can see how the stage is being set for this predicted Russian/Islamic invasion of Israel.

Gog is an exception on Ezekiel's list. Gog is not one of the descendants of Noah listed in Genesis 10. This name, however, is found eleven times in Ezekiel 38–39. It is not the name of a nation, but rather the title of the ruler of Magog—the prince of Rosh, Meshech, and Tubal—the one who leads the invasion against Israel. In fact, *Gog* means "ruler" or "the man on top." It is clear that Gog is an individual rather than a nation because God addresses him as such several times in this prophecy (Ezekiel 38:14; 39:1). Furthermore, Gog is explicitly called a prince and a ruler in Ezekiel 38:2 and 39:1.

THE INVASION OF ISRAEL

ROSH

MAGOG

MESHECH, TUBAL, GOMER

PERSIA

PUT

CUSH

ISRAEL

I n October 2007, during Russian president Vladimir Putin's first-ever visit to Iran, an Iranian newspaper reported that he "reassured Iran that the Bushehr nuclear reactor, a billion dollar energy project being built by Russia and dogged by delays would be completed." The report went on to suggest "maybe the most important result of Putin's trip is to show the independence of Russia toward America and the West."[11] Putin made other first-time-ever visits of a Russian leader to the Muslim nations of Saudi Arabia, Qatar, Jordan, United Arab Emirates, Indonesia, and, most recently, Libya. By all reports, his visits were successful financially, resulting in lucrative agreements and contracts for further joint efforts in the production of oil and the exploration of natural gas reserves.

Apparently the Russian president was successful politically as well. In Libya, President Gadhafi and Putin agreed that the United Nations "needs to be reformed in order to face an 'imbalance of forces' internationally," and especially "the Security Council with which we can work together to resolve problems. In other words, by working together they could remove the veto power held by the U.S. and be able to advance their mutual causes."[12]

> As the mother bear regains her strength, she is actively seeking to draw her brood back into her den.

When will Israel be invaded?

E zekiel does not give a specific date for the invasion, but he does give us ways to identify the time when it will occur: "After many days . . . in the latter years . . ." (Ezekiel 38:8); "On that day when My people of Israel dwell safely . . ." (v. 14); "It will be in the latter days that I will bring you against my land" (v. 16).

The prophet tells us that the invasion of Israel will take place sometime in the future "latter years". It will happen at a time when Israel is dwelling in peace and safety and not involved in conflict with other nations.

Has there ever been such a time in Israel's history? No, there has not. Is today such a time? No! When will there be such a time? The only period in Israel's life that meets this requirement is the time immediately following the Rapture of the church when the Antichrist and the European Union make a treaty with Israel to guarantee her peace and security. When this treaty is signed, the people of Israel will relax the diligence they have been forced to maintain since the founding of their nation in 1948. They will rely on the treaty and turn their attention away from defense to concentrate on increasing their wealth. Israel will truly be a land of unwalled villages. Her defenses will be down, and she will be woefully unprepared for the invasion by the armies of Russia and the coalition.

> The nation of Israel is a democratic republic surrounded by twenty-two hostile Arab/Islamic dictatorships that are 640 times her size and 60 times her population.

What is the purpose of the invasion of Israel?

There are three primary goals for the future invasion of Israel. The first goal will be to seize her land. As Ezekiel puts it, "to stretch out your hand against the waste places that are again inhabited" (Ezekiel 38:12). The second goal of the invaders will be to steal Israel's wealth: "to take plunder and to take booty, to stretch out your hand . . . against a people gathered from the nations, who have acquired livestock and goods, who dwell in the midst of the land . . . to carry away silver and gold, to take away livestock and goods, to take great plunder" (vv. 12–13).

And there is plenty of wealth to be plundered in modern Israel, as we can see by the following quote from a recent article in the *Jerusalem Post*: "Despite a population of only slightly more than 7 million people . . . Israel is now home to more than 7,200 millionaires. . . . Of the 500 wealthiest people in the world, six are now Israeli, and all told, Israel's rich had assets in 2007 of more than $35 billion. . . . Israel's GDP is almost double that of any other Middle East country."[13]

According to one "prosperity index," Israel exported goods and services of more than $70 billion in 2008 including $34.2 billion from the technology sector alone. "Israel is the highest-ranking Middle Eastern country in the index."[14]

Finally, the invading nations have as their ultimate goal the wholesale slaughter of Israel's people: "I will go to a peaceful people, who dwell safely, all of them dwelling without walls, and having neither bars nor gates . . . to stretch out your hand . . . against a people gathered from the nations . . . You will come up against My people Israel like a cloud, to cover the land." (Ezekiel 38:11, 12, 16). The accumulated historical hatred for the Jews will drive these armies forward with the assurance that, this time, the people of Israel will not escape death.

What is God's purpose in the
war and destruction described
in Ezekiel's prophecy?

To understand what is going on in the war and destruction described in Ezekiel's prophecy, we must first consider the sovereignty of God's plan. Even in the most devastating of times, God is still in control. In fact, He often orchestrates events to bring about His purposes. He tells us what He will do to Israel's enemies in no uncertain terms: "I will turn you around, put hooks into your jaws, and lead you out, with all your army, horses, and horsemen" (Ezekiel 38:4); "It will be in the latter days that I will bring you against My land." (v. 16); "I will turn you around and lead you on, bringing you up from the far north, and bring you against the mountains of Israel" (Ezekiel 39:2).

The Old Testament, especially, is intended to show that God is the sovereign ruler over all. Even though men try to thwart His plan and wreak great destruction, God's purpose will always win out. When Ezekiel says that God will bring the enemy against His land, he is simply saying that God will bring these nations to the doom which their wickedness inevitably demands. Everyone accomplishes God's will in the end. Those who conform to His will accomplish it willingly; those who do not conform accomplish it inadvertently as an unwitting tool in His hands.

God's purpose in the cataclysmic battle of the last days is very clear and very simple. God intends for people to recognize Him as the Lord God of heaven whose name is holy, whose glory fills the universe, and whom men must recognize as sovereign if they are to find the peace and joy He desires for His people.

As Ezekiel shows us so vividly, God's destruction of the Axis of Evil in the last days will accomplish the salvation of His people, the nation of Israel. By identifying this Axis of Evil as modern nations who are unwittingly bent on fulfilling this devastating prophecy, we can clearly see how present events will lead to the ultimate accomplishment of God's purposes.

> ## What does *Islam* mean and how many followers does it have?

The name *Islam* literally means "submission." A Muslim is "one who submits to God." According to conservative estimates, there are about 1.5 billion Muslims in our world today. Approximately 1.4 million live in the United States, which is about 6 percent of the U.S. adult population. While we usually associate Islam with the Middle East, the largest Muslim populations are actually in Asia.[15]

> While the majority of the world's 1.5 billion Muslims want no part of the deadly violence and attempt to live in peace with their neighbors, the number of radicals who preach violence and terror is mushrooming around the world.

What is the history of Islam?

According to Islamic tradition, the founder of Islam, Mohammad, was born in Mecca (in present-day Saudi Arabia) in AD 570. Mohammad's father died before the prophet was born, and his mother died when he was six years old. He was raised by his paternal grandfather, grew up to become a camel driver and then a merchant, and, at the age of twenty-six, married a wealthy caravan owner named Khadija.

Mohammad worked in professions that brought him into contact with a number of Christians and Jews who caused him to question the religion of his own people. He was forty years old and meditating in a cave outside Mecca when he received his first revelation. From that moment on, according to his testimony, God occasionally revealed messages to him, which he declared to the people. These messages, which Mohammad received throughout his life, form the verses of the Qu'ran, which Muslims regard as the divine word of God.

In the seventh century Arabian world of Mohammad, the people worshiped over 360 different gods, one for each day of the lunar year. One of these was the moon god, the male counterpart to the female sun god. The moon god was called by various names, one of which was Allah, and it was the favorite god of Mohammad's family.

As Mohammad began to promote his new religion, it was only natural that he would choose to elevate the moon god Allah and declare him to be the one true God. His devotion to Allah was single-minded and fierce, and in establishing and spreading his religion of Islam, Mohammad slaughtered thousands of people who resisted conversion. As his instructions to his followers show, there was no subtlety in his evangelistic technique: "Who relinquishes his faith, kill him . . . I have been ordered by Allah to fight with people till they testify there is no god but Allah, and M[o]hammad is his messenger."[16]

Who are the Shi'ites and the Sunnis, and why are they a threat to Christians?

Opposition in Mecca forced Mohammad and his followers to flee to Medina in AD 620, where he became the head of the first Muslim community. In AD 631 he returned to Mecca, where he died the following year. At his death the Islamic community became bitterly divided over the question of who would be Mohammad's successor. Even today that division survives in the two Islamic sects, now known as the Shi'ites and the Sunnis. Conflict between these sects is one of the major stress points in Iraq and throughout the Islamic world.

At the death of Mohammad, the group we know as the Sunni followed the leadership of Abu Bakr, one of Mohammad's fathers-in-law. The Sunni now comprise about 90 percent of the Islamic world. They believe that Mohammad's spiritual gifts died with him and that their only authority today is the Qu'ran. The Baath party of Saddam Hussein was part of the Sunni sect.

The Shi'ites maintained that Mohammad passed

on a legacy of personal authority in addition to the Qu'ran, as author Winfried Corduan explains:

The Shi'ites, on the other hand, identified with Muhammad's son-in-law Ali, whom they saw as possessing a spiritual endowment directly from the prophet. The Shi'ites believe that their leaders, the imams, have authority on par with the Qu'ran. It is the Shi'ites that believe that the 12th imam went into concealment hundreds of years ago and continues to live there until he returns as the Mahdi . . . the Muslim Messiah![17]

Abu Bakr succeeded Mohammad, and he and his successors launched jihads, or holy wars, that spread the religion of Islam from northern Spain to India and threatened Christian Europe. Christians resisted the threat, and a series of wars followed that drove the Islamic invaders back into the Middle Eastern countries, where they still dominate. Their zeal to have their religion dominate the world has not diminished, however, and it remains a threat to all who do not maintain vigilance.

What does *jihad* mean?

The most frightening word associated with Islam is *jihad*. Sometimes called the "sixth pillar" of Islam, *jihad* actually means "struggle." The greater jihad is the inner struggle of each Muslim to submit to Allah. The lesser jihad is the outward struggle to defend the Islamic community. This is the jihad that strikes fear in the heart of Islamic enemies. Militant Muslims take jihad to mean more than just passive defense of Islam; to them it authorizes the expansion of the Islamic religion even by means of deadly aggression.

The overt hatred for the West expressed in jihad has already spawned many deadly attacks, and the fanaticism that produced them has not diminished. In her book, completed only days before her assassination, former Prime Minister of Pakistan Benazir Bhutto wrote that one of the primary aims of the militants is:

> to provoke a clash of civilizations between the West and . . . Islam. The great hope of the militants is a collision, an explosion between the values of the West and what the extremists claim

to be the values of Islam. . . . The attacks on September 11, 2001, heralded the . . . dream of bloody confrontation . . . If the fanatics and extremists prevail . . . then a great *fitna* (disorder through schism or division) would sweep the world. Here lies their ultimate goal: chaos.[18]

The hatred that the Muslims have for the Jews needs no documentation. But the settlement of Israel into her homeland in 1948 took this hatred to a level of murderous fury. The militants and radicals refer to Israel as "little Satan" and the United States as "big Satan", and they are determined to wipe both countries off the map.

What is *fatah*?

We can easily see and resist the effects of jihad in militant terrorism, but we have trouble seeing and resisting the more subtle strategy that the Muslims call *fatah*. *Fatah* is infiltration, moving into a country in numbers large enough to affect the culture. It means taking advantage of tolerant laws and accommodative policies to insert the influence of Islam. In places where a military invasion will not succeed, the slow, systematic, and unrelenting methods of *fatah* are conquering whole nations. An illustration is:

A demographic revolution is taking place today in France. Some experts are projecting that by the year 2040, 80 percent of the population of France will be Muslim. At that point the Muslim majority will control commerce, industry, education, and religion. They will also control the government, as well, and occupy all the key positions in the French Parliament. And a Muslim will be president.[19]

What are other terms used to describe the Islamic goal of world domination?

Other terms used to describe the Islamic goal of world domination are *biological jihad* or *demographic jihad*, which describe the nonviolent strategy of Muslims moving into Europe and the West and having more babies than their hosts. Within several generations they hope to repopulate traditionally Christian cultures with their own people, and they are certainly on track to reach that goal. According to a Vatican report issued recently, the Roman Catholic Church understands this: "For the first time in history, we are no longer at the top: Muslims have overtaken us."[20]

Does Islam hope to return its Messiah?

The answer to this is a resounding *yes!* This Islamic hope surfaced in a speech by Iranian President Mahmoud Ahmadinejad, a disciple of Ayatollah Khomeni, the cleric who launched the successful 1979 revolution that turned Iran into a strict Islamic state. In 2005, Ahmadinejad was called before the United Nations Security Council to explain his continued determination to develop nuclear weapons. He began his speech by declaring: "In the Name of the God of Mercy, Compassion, Peace, Freedom, and Justice . . . ," and he ended his speech with this prayer: "I pray to you to hasten the emergence of your last repository, the promised one, that perfect and pure human being, the one that will fill this world with justice and peace."[21] The "promised one" in Ahmadinejad's prayer was a reference to the Twelfth Imam, a figure in Shi'ite teaching that parallels the figure of Al-Mahdi in Sunni teaching. In essence, both of these titles refer to the Islamic messiah who is yet to come.

Shi'ia Islam believes that the Twelfth Imam can

appear only during a time of worldwide chaos. This explains many of Ahmadinejad's defiant actions—why he presses forward with his nuclear program in spite of world censure and why he is adamant about destroying Israel. In his infamous speech of October 25, 2005, he said, "'Israel must be wiped off the map', and he warned leaders of Muslim nations who recognized the state of Israel that they would face 'the wrath of their own people.'"[22] With these defiant and divisive actions, Ahmadinejad is fomenting the chaotic environment that he believes will induce the Islamic messiah to come. In a televised speech in 2008, Ahmadinejad reiterated: "What we have right now is the last chapter . . . Accept that the life of Zionists will sooner or later come to an end."[23] On March 14, Ahmadinejad "swept the nation-wide ballot with about 70 percent support."[24]

The world as a whole does not seem to be taking Ahmadinejad seriously, but the people of Israel are an exception. They understand that he is determined to destroy them. And the words of the prophet Ezekiel back up that understanding. He tells us that Iran's (Iran is now the name of the biblical Persia) hatred toward the Jewish nation will play an important role in a major end-time battle.

The Rapture

To Take His Church Home

CHRIST'S COMING IS FAST APPROACHING. IT SEEMS THAT ALL THE PROPHECIES WHICH MUST BE COMPLETED BEFORE HIS RETURN HAVE BEEN FULFILLED. THE LORD WILL DESCEND WITH A SHOUT AND THE TRUMPET OF GOD. ALL BELIEVERS, LIVING AND DEAD, WILL SUDDENLY MEET THE LORD IN THE AIR. LIKE AN EAGER BRIDE, THE CHURCH WAITS FOR THE FINAL CULMINATION OF THE UNION WITH HER GROOM.

As bad as it is today in our world, it could (and will) get worse. A restraining influence in our world holds this evil—this dark satanic tide of perversion and lawlessness—in check. Who has the power to restrain Satan? Only God. And it is God the Holy Spirit, the third person of the Trinity, who draws the line today and keeps the ocean of evil at bay.

Until Christ Returns

What is the Rapture?

According to my online dictionary, the word *rapture* means "an expression or manifestation of ecstasy or passion" and "being carried away by overwhelming emotion."[25] But the Bible tells us it means that millions of people will disappear from the face of the earth in less than a millisecond. And the purpose of that evacuation is to avoid horrific devastation. This evacuation will remove God's people from the disastrous effects of coming earthquakes, fire, and global chaos.

The word *Rapture* is the Latin version of a phrase the Bible uses to describe the catching away of all Christians before the end times. The Lord will descend with a shout and a trumpet of God. All believers, living and dead, will suddenly meet the Lord in the air.

The focus of the Rapture is on looking at the event not from the viewpoint of those who remain, but from that of those who are evacuated. Before the period of the Tribulation breaks out, all true followers of the Lord will be caught up from the earth and right into the presence of the Lord. The Rapture will fulfill the promise He made to His disciples in John 14:1–3:

Let not your heart be troubled; you believe in God, believe also in Me. In My Father's house are many mansions; if it were not so, I would have told you. I go to prepare a place for you. And if I go and prepare a place for you, I will come again and receive you to Myself; that where I am, there you may be also.

Followers of Christ who are raptured will be spared the trauma of death and the coming disasters that will occur when the Tribulation breaks out upon the earth. That is indeed a cause for true rapture on the part of those who love the Lord and long to be with Him.

The New Testament indicates that the Rapture of those who have put their trust in Christ is the next major event on the prophetic calendar. In other words, the Rapture awaits us on the horizon . . . it could happen at any moment. This is the clear message of the Bible, and it is a truth I have taught consistently throughout my years of ministry.

A lot of misunderstanding comes from confusing these two events. When we talk about the signs that signal the return of Christ, we speak not of the Rapture, but of the Lord's ultimate return to the earth with all His saints. According to the book of Revelation, this coming of Christ occurs after the Rapture and differs from it in at least two ways.

First, the Rapture will be a "stealth event" in which Christ will be witnessed by believers only. His Second Coming, on the other hand, will be a public event. Everyone will see Him: "Behold, He is coming with clouds, and every eye will see Him: even they who pierced Him. And all the tribes of the earth will mourn because of Him" (Revelation 1:7; see also Zechariah 14:1, 3–5, Revelation 19:1–21).

Second, all believers are raptured. Jesus will immediately take them back into heaven with Him. But when Christ returns to earth seven years later in the

Second Coming, He is coming to stay. This return, usually referred to as "the Second Advent," will take place at the end of the Tribulation period and usher in the Millennium—a thousand-year reign of Christ on this earth. So, first, the Rapture will occur seven years before the Second Advent. At that time Christ will take us to be with Him in heaven, immediately before the seven-year Tribulation period. Then, secondly, we will return to earth with Him at His Second Advent.

There is another important difference. There are no events that must take place before the Rapture occurs. It's all a matter of God's perfect timing. When I preach that signs are developing concerning the Lord's return, I'm referring to events that must yet occur before the return of Christ in the Second Advent.

> As bad as things are becoming, we can hardly overstate the horror that will occur when society loses the tempering influence of Christians.

What does the apostle Paul say about the Rapture?

In this passage Paul tells us all we need to know about the Rapture:

> But I do not want you to be ignorant, brethren, concerning those who have fallen asleep, lest you sorrow as others who have no hope. For if we believe that Jesus died and rose again, even so God will bring with Him those who sleep in Jesus.
>
> For this we say to you by the word of the Lord, that we who are alive and remain until the coming of the Lord will by no means precede those who are asleep. For the Lord Himself will descend from heaven with a shout, with the voice of an archangel, and with the trumpet of God. And the dead in Christ will rise first. Then we who are alive and remain shall be caught up together with them in the clouds to meet the Lord in the air. And thus we shall always be with the Lord. Therefore comfort one another with these words (1 Thessalonians 4:13–18).

First, Paul wrote: "But I do not want you to be ignorant, brethren, concerning those who have fallen asleep, lest you sorrow as others who have no hope" (1 Thessalonians 4:13). In this passage the apostle addresses the ignorance of the Thessalonians concerning the state of those who had died believing in Christ. The word he used to describe that state has great significance for every believer today. Paul said that they had fallen *asleep*. For the word translated *asleep*, he used the Greek word *koimaw*, which has as one of its meanings "to sleep in death." The same word is used to describe the deaths of Lazarus, Stephen, David, and Jesus Christ.

Lazarus: "These things He said, and after that He said to them, 'Our friend Lazarus *sleeps*, but I go that I may wake him up'" (John 11:11 emphasis added).

Stephen: "Then he [Stephen] knelt down and cried out with a loud voice 'Lord, do not charge them with this sin.' And when he had said this, he *fell asleep*" (Acts 7:60 emphasis added).

David: "For David, after he had served his own generation by the will of God, *fell asleep*, was buried with his fathers, and saw corruption" (Acts 13:36 emphasis added).

Jesus Christ: "But now Christ is risen from the dead, and has become the firstfruits of those who have fallen *asleep*" (1 Corinthians 15:20 emphasis added).

This concept of death is emphasized in the wonderful word early Christians adopted for the burying places of their loved ones. It was the Greek word *koimeterion*, which means "a rest house for strangers, a sleeping place." It is the word from which we get our English word *cemetery*. In Paul's day this word was used for inns, or what we would call a hotel or motel. We check in at a Hilton Hotel or a Ramada Inn expecting to spend the night in sleep before we wake up in the morning refreshed and raring to go. That is exactly the thought Paul expresses in words such as *koimaw* and *koimeterion*. When Christians die, it's as if they are slumbering peacefully in a place of rest, ready to be awakened at the return of the Lord. The words have great import, for they convey the Christian concept of death not as a tragic finality, but as a temporary sleep.

In the next part of the Thessalonians passage, we find Paul affirming their hope that their loved ones will live again. He does this by tying that hope to the Resurrection and the Rapture: "lest you sorrow as others who have no hope. For if we believe that Jesus died and rose again, even so God will bring with Him those who sleep in Jesus" (1 Thessalonians 4:13–14). Here Paul tells the Thessalonians (and us) that God's plan for our future gives us such a new perspective on death that when someone we love dies, we are not overcome with sorrow and despair, for on that day when those who are alive in Christ are raptured, those who died in Christ will be raised to be with Him.

Will Christ return at the Rapture?

P aul states in 1 Thessalonians, "For the Lord Himself will descend from heaven with a shout, with the voice of an archangel, and with the trumpet of God" (v. 4:16). As you read these words, the Lord Jesus Christ is seated in the heavens at the right hand of the Almighty Father. But when the right moment comes, Jesus will initiate the Rapture by literally and physically rising from the throne, stepping into the corridors of light, and actually descending into the atmosphere of planet earth from which He rose into the heavens over the Mount of Olives two thousand years ago. It is not the angels or the Holy Spirit, but the Lord Himself who is coming to draw believers into the heavens in the Rapture.

Who will be resurrected at the Rapture?

Paul says in 1 Thessalonians 4:16, "the dead in Christ will rise first." As he indicates here, the call to resurrection at the Rapture will not summon all the dead, but believers only. A time will come much later when *all* the dead will be raised to stand before the white throne in judgment. But at this first call, our believing loved ones who have already died will arise to take first place in the program of the Rapture.

Paul then explains the next event in the Rapture sequence. "Then we who are alive and remain shall be caught up." (1 Thessalonians 4:17). The words *caught up* are translated from a Greek word which has as one of its meanings "to snatch out or away speedily." This word emphasizes the sudden nature of the Rapture. Paul describes this suddenness in his letter to the Corinthians: "In a moment, in the twinkling of an eye, at the last trumpet. For the trumpet will sound, and the dead will be raised incorruptible, and we shall be changed" (1 Corinthians 15:52).

Paul continues his explanation of the Rapture:

"Then we who are alive and remain shall be caught up together with them [the believing dead who have arisen] in the clouds to meet the Lord in the air. And thus we shall always be with the Lord" (1 Thessalonians 4:17). Note that Paul begins here with the word *then*, which is an adverb indicating sequence. It connects the previous events of the Rapture that we have already considered with this final event in a definite order of sequential reunions as follows:

- Dead bodies reunited with their spirits
- Resurrected believers reunited with living believers
- Resurrected believers and raptured believers meet the Lord

As Paul points out, the ultimate consequence of this reunion with the Lord is that there will be no subsequent parting. After His return, our union and communion with Him will be uninterrupted and eternal. This glorious fact alone shows us why the word *rapture* is an altogether appropriate term for this event.

Will those who have been cremated be a part of the Rapture?

When the Scripture says, "The dead in Christ will rise," it is speaking of the bodily resurrection of *all* believers! At this time, the spirits of believers will be united with their perfect and complete resurrection bodies. "For the Lord Himself will descend from heaven with a shout, with the voice of an archangel, and with the trumpet of God. And the dead in Christ will rise first [no exceptions!]. Then we who are alive and remain shall be caught up together with them in the clouds to meet the Lord in the air. And thus we shall always be with the Lord. Therefore comfort one another with these words" (1 Thessalonians 4:16–18).

What events will take place in heaven after the Rapture?

After the Rapture, we will come before the Judgment Seat of Christ one by one (2 Corinthians 5:10). The Judgment Seat is not about whether we will enter heaven—we'll already be there. It will be a time to give an account of the works we have done on earth, and we will be rewarded accordingly. We'll be assigned places of authority in the coming Millennium based upon our faithfulness to God when we were on earth, as well as the influence we left behind.

Why should I avoid determining a date and time for the Rapture?

The fact is we cannot calculate the day Christ will return because God specifically chose not to reveal it to us.

When the apostles asked Jesus about the end times, He replied gently but firmly, "It is not for you to know times or seasons which the Father has put in His own authority. But you shall receive power when the Holy Spirit has come upon you" (Acts 1:7–8). Only God knows what time it is, and only God knows when these times will run out. God's calendar is the only one that matters (1 Thessalonians 5:1–2; Matthew 24:36, 42, 44, 50; Matthew 25:13).

Future truth impacts present responsibility. It is the knowledge that His coming is soon that puts urgency into our step and determination into our service.

After completing his description of the Rapture to the Thessalonians, Paul wraps up the passage with this practical admonition: "Therefore comfort one another with these words" (1 Thessalonians 4:18).

Here the apostle tells both the Thessalonians and believers today that it's not enough simply to passively understand what he has just explained about the Rapture, Christian death, and the Resurrection. Our understanding should spur us toward a certain action—to "comfort one another." And in the preceding verses He has given us exactly the kind of information that makes true comfort possible. When believers suffer the loss of family members or dearly loved friends, we have in Paul's descriptions of Christian death and resurrection all that is needed to comfort one another in these losses. Christian death is not permanent; it is merely a "sleep." A time is coming when we and our loved ones will be reunited in a rapturous meeting, when Christ Himself calls us out of this world or out of our graves to be with Him forever in an ecstatic relationship of eternal love. That is why Paul tells us we should comfort one another with reminders that, for Christians, what we call death is nothing more than a temporary sleep before we are called into our uninterrupted relationship with Christ forever.

> Christian death is not
> permanent; it is merely a sleep.

> "The entire world will hear the Gospel before Christ returns . . ." "Jesus could come at any time . . ." How can both of these statements be true?

First of all, Jesus could come tonight! But you may hear people say that the Rapture cannot occur until the whole world has heard the Gospel; therefore, we need to preach the Gospel to every creature so that the "last person to be saved" is brought into the kingdom, at which time Jesus will return for His Church. But this cannot be true.

If there is anything that has yet to happen before Christ's return, there is no such thing as the "imminent return" of Jesus Christ. The command to take the Gospel into the whole world is certainly pressing upon every generation, but the condition of the Gospel going to the whole world is a condition not of the Rapture, but of the Second Coming of Christ.

The Tribulation

To Allow Unrestrained Evil

THE MOMENT AFTER THE RAPTURE, the Spirit of God will remove any restraining influence on earth. As a result, life on earth will be relinquished to flourishing evil. As the Tribulation progresses, evil will result in a climax of worsening conditions. God's wrath will be displayed toward the wicked through the signs of His coming judgment. Thankfully, those who are believers at the time of the Rapture will be spared from this terrible time.

The hour-hand on God's time clock is wound up and spinning. We are being swept along the path of history by a swift wind at our backs. Our individual ability to weather the storm will come from our understanding of the Word of God. We need only heed what has echoed through the centuries: "He who has an ear, let him hear what the Spirit says to the churches" (Revelation 3:22).

Escape the Coming Night

What is the Tribulation?

The Tribulation is a seven-year period described in Revelation 11–18. Approximately the first three and a half years of that time, there will be the climax of worsening conditions, the anger of God against the wicked, and the signs of Christ's coming. During the last three and a half years, the "lawless one"—the Antichrist—will be empowered to sit at the center of the Tribulation's evil as he personifies Satan.

What signs will warn of the approaching Tribulation period?

These ten events are the things we can expect in embryonic form in the days preceding the Rapture and the beginning of the Tribulation. These ten things will continue to multiply and progress as the first three and one-half years of the Great Tribulation unfold.

❖ A Time of Deception—"Many will come in My name, saying, 'I am the Christ,' and will deceive many" (Matthew 24:5).

❖ A Time of Dissension—"You will hear of wars and rumors of wars . . . Nation will rise against nation, and kingdom against kingdom" (Matthew 24:6–7).

❖ A Time of Devastation—"There will be famines . . ." (Matthew 24:7).

❖ A Time of Disease—" . . . pestilences . . ." (Matthew 24:7).

❖ A Time of Disasters—" . . . and earthquakes in various places" (Matthew 24:7).

❖ A Time of Death—"They will deliver you up to tribulation and kill you, and you will be hated by all nations for My name's sake" (Matthew 24:9).

❖ A Time of Disloyalty—"Many will be offended, will betray one another, and will hate one another" (Matthew 24:10).

❖ A Time of Delusion—"Many false prophets will rise up and deceive many" (Matthew 24:11). It should also be noted that part of the delusion will be an increase in drug use. One of the characteristics of the end times' false religion will be what the book of Revelation calls "sorceries" (9:21). The word John uses is *pharmakia*, from which we get the word *pharmacy*. It is an ancient reference to the ingestion of drugs. The use of mind-altering substances such as narcotics and hallucinogens will be associated with false religions, doubtless with the approval of the government.

❖ A Time of Defection—"Because lawlessness will abound, the love of many will grow cold" (Matthew 24:12). People will turn away from God and from one another.

❖ A Time of Declaration—"This gospel of the kingdom will be preached in all the world as a witness to all the nations" (Matthew 24:14).

Life on earth will be relinquished to flourishing evil.

What will happen on earth during the Tribulation?

I believe the Tribulation is a natural consequence of the Rapture. You may think the world today is degenerating into rampant greed and immorality, and indeed it is. When all Christians are removed from the earth, the restraining ministry of the Holy Spirit will be completely absent. The result will be horrific. Jesus Himself described what will happen next: "For then there will be great tribulation, such as has not been since the beginning of the world until this time, no, nor ever shall be. And unless those days were shortened, no flesh would be saved" (Matthew 24:21–22).

What will happen in heaven during the Tribulation?

The Christians are in heaven. God is seated on the throne, which is surrounded by a rainbow of emerald greens. The twenty-four elders representing the church-age saints sit around the throne. Before the throne is a sea of glass. In the midst of the throne are the four living creatures, and giving praise around the throne are the angels and the Church (Revelation 4:3–4, 6, 8). This is the worship of the glorified Christ, the Creator of the world. God is just about to deal with the physical earth in judgment, and before He does, the Creator of earth is worshiped by the Church in heaven. Thunder, lightning, and voices signify the judgment which is about to fall on the earth.

Will Christians escape the Tribulation?

C hristians will escape the seven-year nightmare of the Tribulation.

I believe the Bible clearly teaches that one of the coming great events in the fulfillment of prophecy concerns the Church. This is the personal, bodily return of the Lord in the air to remove His waiting Church from the earth and to reward them according to their works. This will take place before the Tribulation period during which time the judgments of God will be poured out upon the unbelieving world.

I believe there are more Scriptures to support the imminent return of Christ for His Church prior to the Tribulation than during or after it: 1 Thessalonians 4:13–18; 2 Thessalonians 2:8–12; 1 Thessalonians 1:10, 5:9.

"Those who are wise will shine like the brightness of the heavens, and those who lead many to righteousness, like the stars for ever and ever" (Daniel 12:3 NIV). In the midst of all the difficult times, the horror of the Tribulation, God has some special things that He has reserved for those who serve Him. He says they are to become like stars in His galaxy!

The Handwriting on the Wall

❖ **The sun will turn black, the moon will turn red, and great earthquakes will be common.**

Revelation 6:12 says, "Behold, there was a great earthquake." It also says, "The sun became black as sackcloth of hair, and the moon became like blood." When Jesus died on the cross, the whole earth became dark at midday. When Egypt was judged, there was a blackness of night. When the Lord came down at Mt. Sinai, the mountain was shrouded in black clouds. The prophets, as well, said darkness would occur at the beginning of the Tribulation period.

❖ **The stars will fall out of the sky.**

"The stars of heaven fell to the earth" (Revelation 6:13). The word *star* here is the Greek word *aster* and it refers to luminous bodies in the sky other than the sun and moon. Clearly these stars are not the distant stellar objects we know as stars but more like a group of asteroids.

❖ **The mountains and islands will move.**

"Every mountain and island was moved out of its place" (Revelation 6:14). When the asteroids hit the earth, the possibility is that the earth's crust will be so disturbed by the impact that great segments of it will actually begin to slip and slide over the earth's mantle. According to Dr. Henry Morris, those living in the regions above such shifting will observe the heavens appearing to move in the opposite direction, as if they are being rolled up.

❖ **The ocean will become blood.**

As Revelation 8:8–9 explains, a great mountain burning with fire will be cast into the sea. One-third of the sea will become blood, and one-third of all sea life will die. There will also be the destruction of one-third of all the ships. The far-reaching implications of these judgments are beyond our understanding. Someone has reasoned that the oceans occupy about three-fourths of the earth's surface, so the extent of this judgment will be staggering. The pollution of the water and the death of so many sea creatures will vastly affect the balance of life in the ocean. This will happen to one-third of the saltwater bodies of the world.

❖ **The water will become poisoned.**

Then the freshwater supplies will be affected. They will become bitter, with the result that many people will die (Revelation 8:10–11). The instrument of judgment will be a great star that is labeled "Wormwood." This literal star or meteor hurtling through space will approach the earth. Sweeping along the surface of the earth, it will turn one-third of the water of the earth into a deadly poisonous liquid. It will affect the rivers, springs, and wells.

This is a time of the greatest suffering and persecution the world has ever seen.

Will people be saved during the Tribulation?

Yes, there will be a great harvest of souls for Christ during the Tribulation. In this harvest of souls, we see fulfilled the prophecy contained in Matthew 24:14—"And this gospel of the kingdom will be preached in all the world as a witness to all the nations, and then the end will come," then the Second Coming of Christ!

People from every nation, tribe, and language will be part of the great redeemed multitude. This is a time of the greatest suffering and persecution the world has ever seen, and it will also be a time when the greatest wave of genuine conversion ever takes place. This multitude of redeemed ones will come from those who were still unsaved at the time of the Rapture.

Today there are at least two billion people who have never heard or understood enough of the gospel to accept or reject it. Those who will be saved during the Tribulation will come from this great number. Those who are saved during the Tribulation will be saved on exactly the same basis as those before the Tribulation, which is by faith in the life, death, and justifying resurrection of the Son of God.

The condition of the Gospel going to the whole world is a condition not of the Rapture, but of the Second Coming of Christ.

Unsolved Mysteries

How will people be saved during the Tribulation?

I f there are no believers on earth at the beginning of the seven years of the Tribulation, this is a good question. As we will discuss in upcoming pages, there will be two witnesses and 144,000 sealed Israelites (Revelation 11:3, 7:4). In addition, Dr. Henry Morris suggests a "silent witness" because "millions upon millions of copies of the Bible and Bible portions . . . will not [be] remove[d] and multitudes will no doubt be constrained to read the Bible in those days . . . [and] will turn to their Creator and Savior." These blood-bought believers will begin to warn others of even more severe judgment to come. They will preach repentance and judgment and they will be killed for their message.

> If people become Christians during the Tribulation, what will happen to them when they die?

T he Lord sends an angel for their own special blessing: "Blessed are the dead who die in the Lord" (Revelation 14:13). Just as the New Testament begins with the Beatitudes of Jesus for the living, it ends with the Beatitude of Jesus for the dying. This is the second of the seven Beatitudes found in the book of Revelation. Even though these words are particularly written for those who die during the Tribulation, they are also written for the saints of every generation, for the dead in Christ of all ages. Believers do not die in the sense of death being the end; they are simply waiting for the coming of the Lord. Blessed are those who have gone to sleep in Jesus.

> If I can be saved during the
> Tribulation, why should I
> change my life now?

J ust as death terminates the day of possible salvation for those who reject Christ, so does the Rapture. Those who have heard the Gospel message and have rejected it will be given a "strong delusion" during the Tribulation. Second Thessalonians 2:10–12 tells us, "they received not the love of the truth, that they might be saved. And for this reason God shall send them a 'strong delusion,' that they should believe the lie." Revelation 13 tells us it will be the lies of the Beast and the Antichrist, who counterfeit the life of Christ and bring deception. Believing these deceptions, the people who have rejected the Gospel before the Tribulation will go to hell without opportunity to receive Christ. The day of grace will be over for them. There is no second chance.

Be warned: You had better not wait to become a Christian. I've heard people reason like this before, but I have to wonder about someone's legitimate desire to know God if it is coupled with a desire to beat the system. Do not let anyone tell you that you can beat the system by waiting to become a Christian until the Tribulation. It won't happen. You'll be deceived. The reason more people aren't saved today is because of deception. It's amazing, but the more the Tribulation grows in intensity, the more people reject God. You'd think they would turn to Him and cry for mercy, but instead they curse Him who sends judgment on the earth. Those who reject the truth now will be deceived and will never believe the Gospel when they hear it preached.

The Bible says today is the day of salvation (2 Corinthians 6:2). Don't try to get around God's plan. Don't think you can beat the system. One day soon the Lord is coming back, and if you have already rejected Him, the day of opportunity will be gone.

> Is it true that it will be impossible for people to kill themselves during the Tribulation?

Even though men will seek to die and suicide will be attempted, apparently death will not be possible: "In those days men will seek death and will not find it; they will desire to die, and death will flee from them" (Revelation 9:6).

It will be such an awful experience for those who are left to endure the result of countless demons from the pit running unchecked throughout the earth. The only people these demons are allowed to sting are those who do not belong to God (v. 4). The poison from the sting will literally set the nerve center on fire (v. 10). This evil will be stretched out for 150 days (v. 10), and death cannot provide escape (v. 6).

When divine restraint is withdrawn during the Tribulation, human passions will break loose, and morality will be discarded in favor of liberty and "sexual immorality" (Revelation 22:15). The result will be nothing less than rampant immorality.

Who are the two witnesses
that will preach the Gospel
during the Tribulation?

I believe the two witnesses are Elijah and Moses. In Malachi 4:5–6, we are told that Elijah will come before Jesus returns. In 1 Kings 17, Elijah stopped the rain; and in Revelation 11:6, the witnesses "have power to shut heaven, so that no rain falls in the days of their prophecy." Another reason I believe it to be Elijah is because Elijah didn't die. Elijah was taken to heaven in a whirlwind of fire.

I believe the second witness to be Moses. In Exodus 7:20 and 21, Moses turned "the water into blood"; and in Revelation 11:6 the two witnesses are said to "have power over waters to turn them to blood." Moses died, but no one knows where his body is buried (Deuteronomy 34:5–6). The body of Moses was preserved by God so that he might be restored. Finally, it is also significant that Elijah appeared with Moses in the Transfiguration.

It is impossible to prove conclusively who these two witnesses are. But if they are not Moses and Elijah, we can know that they are very much like them and have the same kind of ministry.

In these days of crises, our trust should not rest in a nation that may shortly disappear, but in Him who works all things after the counsel of His own will.

~Herman A. Hoyt

When will these witnesses appear?

I n Revelation 11:3, we are introduced to the two witnesses. There is much debate as to when these
witnesses appear on the scene. I believe they begin their
ministry at the beginning of the Tribulation, at the time
the Antichrist makes his covenant with the Jewish
people. We can assume they will have a great following.

What special powers will the two witnesses possess?

Revelation 11:5 says, "If anyone wants to harm them, fire proceeds from their mouth and devours their enemies." God has provided them with protection. These witnesses will have power over death, drought, and disease.

They will preach about Christ as Lord of all the earth. They will shut the heavens so no rain can fall during their ministry, and they will have power to cause plagues as often as they desire. They will go about testifying of the wickedness of the people. They will tell the people that God is responsible for all the judgments that have been poured out. If that is not enough, they will tell them of more terrifying judgments to come. They will preach against the Beast of Revelation 13, and men try to destroy them because their witness exposes the wickedness of the earth.

What will happen to the witnesses?

After forty-two months, during which time they cannot be killed, they will be killed by the Beast who ascends from the bottomless pit. The two witnesses are so hated that the entire world will rejoice at their deaths. Their bodies will be put on public display. Their bodies will lie in the street for three and a half days (Revelation 11:7–10). In biblical Jewish society this was an abomination. Their enemies will be ecstatic that someone has finally put an end to these two nemeses.

They are already decomposing, and the next action we see is that they stand up! The whole world will see this because they are looking in on the scene through the news and the papers. While they are the focus of world attention, they are not only resurrected, they are raptured (Revelation 11:12). They go up to heaven in "a cloud." This cloud is the *shekinah* glory of God. It is the same cloud in which the angel of Revelation 10:1 was clothed.

The Antichrist

Satan's Superman

WHEN I FIRST BEGAN STUDYING PROPHECY NEARLY FORTY YEARS AGO, I ENCOUNTERED THE BIBLE'S PREDICTION THAT ONE MAN WOULD EVENTUALLY TAKE CONTROL OF THE ENTIRE WORLD. FRANKLY, I COULD NOT IMAGINE HOW SUCH A THING WOULD EVER HAPPEN. BUT SINCE THE BIBLE PRESENTED THIS AS A MAJOR PART OF THE END-TIME LANDSCAPE, I BELIEVED IT AND I PREACHED IT EVEN THOUGH I COULD NOT COMPREHEND IT.

As civilization speeds toward its final destiny, the appearance of a powerful world ruler is inevitable.

LaHaye and Hindson, *Global Warning*

> If Satan was defeated at the cross, why does he still have so much power, both now and into the future?

The ultimate victory has been won at Calvary, but it will be implemented in the future. The sentence has been passed, now it needs to be enforced. The enforcement is in the hands of the Church. The tool that enforces Satan's defeat is the tool of prayer. "For the weapons of our warfare are not carnal but mighty in God for pulling down strongholds, casting down arguments and every high thing that exalts itself against the knowledge of God, bringing every thought into captivity to the obedience of Christ" (2 Corinthians 10:4–5). One person praying on earth can move angels in heaven.

Christians need to learn the power of prayer against Satan and that he will be defeated in his work. We are not engaged in the warfare if we are not praying against Satan. The judgment that was effected at the cross, and is enforced through prayer, will be completed. Satan is doomed. Once our warfare with Satan is ended by the Rapture, he will be unobstructed in his evil plans. But, make no mistake, Satan and his henchmen—the Antichrist and the false prophet—will keep their divine appointment with Almighty God. Satan, already defeated, is doomed.

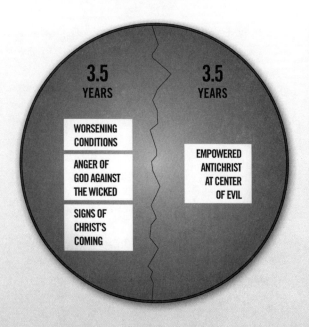

Who is the Antichrist?

The Antichrist is a person who is against Christ. The prefix *anti* can also mean "instead of," and both meanings will apply to this coming world leader. He will overtly oppose Christ and at the same time pass himself off as Christ.

The Antichrist will aggressively live up to his terrible name. He will be Satan's superman who persecutes, tortures, and kills the people of God and leads the armies of the world into the climactic Battle of Armageddon. He will be the most powerful dictator the world has ever seen, making Caesar, Hitler, Mao, and Saddam seem weak and tame by comparison.

Even though the Antichrist is identified by that name only four times in the Bible, he appears many more times under various aliases. He is also called:

- ❖ "the prince that shall come"—Daniel 9:26 NKJV
- ❖ "a fierce king"—Daniel 8:23
- ❖ "a master of intrigue"—Daniel 8:23 NIV
- ❖ "a despicable man"—Daniel 11:21 NLT

- ❖ "a worthless shepherd"—Zechariah 11:16–17 NLT
- ❖ "the one who brings destruction"—
  2 Thessalonians 2:3 NLT
- ❖ "the lawless one"—2 Thessalonians 2:8 NKJV
- ❖ "the evil man"—2 Thessalonians 2:9 NLT
- ❖ "the Beast"—Revelation 13:1 NKJV

When he comes on the scene, people will flock to him like flies to honey, and they will fall over themselves to do anything he asks.

Satan is the first person and the father of the unholy trinity. The Antichrist is the second person and the son of the unholy trinity. While the Holy Spirit is the third person of the Trinity and His main function is to direct praise to the person of Christ, the False Prophet's major function is to direct the worship and praise of the people back to the Antichrist (Revelation 13:11–12).

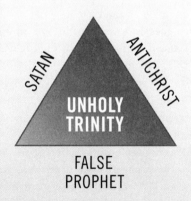

What are some characteristics of the Antichrist?

The prophet Daniel describes the Antichrist in these graphic terms: "After this I saw in the night visions, and behold, a fourth beast . . . And there . . . were eyes like the eyes of a man, and a mouth speaking pompous words. . . . He shall speak pompous words against the Most High" (Daniel 7:7–8, 25).

As Daniel says, the coming world leader will be renowned for this kind of eloquence, which will capture the attention and admiration of the world.

Daniel goes on to tell us that not only will this golden-tongued orator speak in high-blown terms, but he will also utter pompous words against the Most High. The apostle John describes him in a similar fashion in the book of Revelation: "And he was given a mouth speaking great things and blasphemies" (Revelation 13:5).

Daniel continues his description of the Antichrist by telling us he is a man "whose appearance was greater than his fellows" (Daniel 7:20). In terms of his outward appearance, this man will be a strikingly attractive person. The combination of magnetic personality, speaking ability, and extreme good looks will make him virtually irresistible to the masses. When he comes on the scene, people will flock to him like flies to honey, and they will fall over themselves to do anything he asks. The apostle John expands on Daniel's description of the Antichrist's blasphemous acts by telling us that every living person will be required to worship this man. "He was granted power to give breath to the image of the beast, that the image of the beast should both speak and cause as many as would not worship the image of the beast to be killed" (Revelation 13:15).

Finally, Revelation 13:1–8 says the Antichrist is represented as a Beast—an appropriate title for him. During the last three and a half years of the Tribulation, the Antichrist will personify Satan himself. Second Thessalonians 2:9 says, "The coming of the lawless one is according to the working of Satan, with all power, signs, and lying wonders." Step by step, the Antichrist will promote himself from a European leader, to a world leader, to a tyrannical global dictator, and finally to a god.

How does the Antichrist gain political power?

His rise to power is inconspicuous. It will not be noticed in the beginning and will hardly raise the attention even of those who are closest to the center of action. He will rise out of the general population. John says, "Then I stood on the sand of the sea. And I saw a beast rising up out of the sea, having seven heads and ten horns" (Revelation 13:1). The sea in biblical imagery stands for the general mass of humanity or, more specifically, the Gentile nations.

Whatever power the Antichrist has, he only has it by virtue of the fact that he is allowed to have it by Almighty God. As bad as the Tribulation is, it is never out of God's control. There is a leash on Satan, and God is holding on to the other end of the leash. Satan will be able to do only that which God allows him to do in the Tribulation period.

The combination of magnetic
personality, speaking ability, and
extreme good looks will make
him virtually irresistible to the
masses.

Who will worship the Antichrist?

According to Revelation 13:8, "all who dwell on the earth will worship him." Daniel 7:25 tells us that the Antichrist is a cultic leader. "He shall speak pompous words against the Most High . . . and shall intend to change times and law." He will speak out against the true God of heaven. The language suggests that he will try to raise himself to the level of God and make declarations from that position.

Second Thessalonians 2:4 says the Antichrist ". . . opposes and exalts himself above all that is called God or that is worshiped, so that he sits as God in the temple of God, showing himself that he is God." He will accept the worship of the peoples of the world.

What is the mark of the Beast?

The mark of the Beast is 666. We can't identify the exact significance of the mark, but there are some general things we can say about it. The number six is the number of man (Revelation 13:18). Man was created on the sixth day. He is to work six out of seven days. A Hebrew slave could not be enslaved more than six years. Their fields could not be sown for more than six years running. The number 666 is man-tripled. Perhaps the number of the Beast represents the ultimate in human ingenuity and competence.

The word used for the mark of the Beast is the Greek word *charagma*. In antiquity, this word was always associated with the Roman emperor. It often contained the Emperor's name, his effigy, and the year of his reign. It was necessary for buying and selling, and it was required to be affixed to documents to attest to their validity. The Antichrist will do the same thing. "He causes all, both small and great, rich and poor, free and slave, to receive a mark on their right hand or on their foreheads, and that no one may buy or sell except one who has the mark or the name of the beast, or the number of his name" (Revelation 13:16–17).

Those who refuse the mark of the Beast will be persecuted and labeled as traitors. According to the system organized by the Beast, everyone who does not wear the mark will be denied the ability to buy or sell (Revelation 13:16–17). Apparently, this will lead to their death as they will not even be able to get the food and other things necessary to stay alive.

> What will happen to those who take the mark of the Beast?

Revelation 14:9–11 warns that all who receive the mark of the Beast will suffer eternal judgment at the hand of God. In this passage, the angel announces that those who take the mark of the beast will be consigned to eternal fire, damnation, and wrath. Their torment will last forever since they have chosen to worship and serve the Beast rather than the one true God.

How will the Beast be defeated?

S atan allows the Beast to be killed—or at least to appear to be killed. But the head wound he receives will be healed, and the world will be so astonished they will follow him (Revelation 13:3–4,12). Once again the imitator is at work. He will feign the Resurrection. This is Satan's last fling. He will use everything at his disposal to take as many people to hell with him as he can.

Just when it seems there is no hope, the Lord will return in His Second Coming to dethrone the Beast at the Battle of Armageddon. The nations and Israel will then be judged, and Christ will institute the Millennium.

Who is the False Prophet?

The False Prophet is a man who exercises religious and military authority in the name of the Antichrist. He does miraculous things to cause the whole world to bow down and worship the Antichrist and his image. Jesus says in Matthew 7:15, "Beware of false prophets, who come to you in sheep's clothing, but inwardly they are ravenous wolves." The False Prophet in Revelation is the epitome of every false prophet who has gone before him. We need to be warned against false prophets who come with the voice and personality and calmness of a lamb, but who speak the words of Satan himself.

What will the False Prophet look like?

According to Revelation 13:11, he has the voice of a dragon, but he looks like a lamb. Why would Satan design the False Prophet to look like a lamb? He is continuing to do everything possible to deceive people by counterfeiting the ministry of Jesus, the Lamb of God who was slain before the foundation of the world (Revelation 13:8).

What powers will the False Prophet have?

The False Prophet will be the Antichrist's religious leader and will have the power to counterfeit the miracles of God according to Revelation 13:13. The specific miracle mentioned in the text is the calling down of fire from heaven. The False Prophet may be trying to imitate Elijah, when he called down fire on Mount Carmel, to make people think he *is* Elijah who is coming before the great and terrible day of the Lord. He deceives people into building an image as a central point of worship for the Beast (v. 14). With his occultic powers, he will enable the image to speak (v. 15).

What is the significance of the 144,000 Israelites mentioned in Revelation?

During the Tribulation, God will send His two witnesses into the world to prophesy and perform mighty miracles. There will also be 144,000 Israelites "sealed" for God's service during this period (Revelation 7:4). The 144,000 Israelites—12,000 from each of the twelve tribes of Israel—will become evangelists and shall see a great harvest of souls during these terrible Tribulation days. They will be preserved so that they cannot be killed, and people will hear their message and be saved. It is hard to imagine the impact 144,000 Spirit-filled Jews might have on the world. Their power from the Holy Spirit enables them to have great courage and bravery as they give witness to the Word and testify to salvation in Jesus Christ. Twelve Spirit-filled Jews turned their world upside down. Imagine the magnitude of the revival that will take place during the Tribulation.

What does the Bible mean by 144,000 virgins?

In Revelation 14:4 the word *virgin* is not a physical description. As we see in 2 Corinthians 11:2, the church must be presented to Jesus Christ as a chaste virgin. The idea is not about physical virginity but has everything to do with spiritual virginity. The church must be holy. Likewise, in Revelation 14:4 the word refers to the fact that the 144,000 will be separated from the corruption of the world. They will be virgins unto God who give themselves in pure devotion to the Lord. They will be a truly separated and sanctified group of people, unsoiled by the pollution of the world. That's the kind of witness God craves, no matter what generation we live in. The more holy we are, the more God can use us. Perhaps the greatest preparation we can make for ministry is the preparation of our own hearts in righteousness and holiness before God.

What does it mean when the Bible says the 144,000 are sealed with the mark of God?

Revelation 7:3–4 explains that the 144,000 evangelists will be sealed on their foreheads and preserved in their ministry by the Spirit of God. They will have the Father's name written prominently on their foreheads.

It is death not to have the mark of the Beast written on one's head during the time of the Tribulation. But during the Tribulation, 144,000 people will be walking around *without* 666 written on them, and they will not be killed. They will not be neutral; they will be aggressive. They won't just be walking around without the mark; they'll be walking around with their own mark. They don't want anyone to be in doubt as to who they belong to. They have God's mark on them, and it will be evident to everyone.

It is death to have the mark of God, but these preachers confess Christ and are unashamed of Him. And they are preserved. They have come all the way through the Tribulation preaching the gospel. They are all still alive. God sealed them. When you are God's person, in God's will, you are immortal until God is finished with you. God is in control. That doesn't mean that you should live life recklessly, but it means that God has committed Himself to preserve you through-out your ministry.

Will there be consequences
on earth for those who
worship the Beast?

Revelation 16:2 gives us the record of terrible sores upon those who have taken the mark of the Beast and worshiped his image. The sores reflected on these rebels symbolize that they worship Satan.

Those who have taken the mark of the Beast appear to be religious people. They identify with the great religious regime of their day. But in this awful moment of judgment when the bowls are turned over on earth, the sores will be another mark of identification to demonstrate that they are rebelling against God. It's as if God causes the poison of the rebellion within these people to surface and be manifested in sores all over their bodies.

At this time, God will use six other disasters on earth to carry out His judgment. The remaining part of the sea will turn to blood, rivers and streams will become blood, the sun will scorch people with fire, the earth will be in darkness, the Euphrates River will completely dry up, and thunder, lightning, and hailstones weighing nearly one hundred pounds will fall from the sky (Revelation 16:3–21 NIV).

The Antichrist will aggressively live up to his terrible name. He will be Satan's Superman, who persecutes, tortures, and kills the people of God and leads the armies of the world into the climactic battle of Armageddon.

> Will those who worship the Antichrist experience anything like the Old Testament plagues in Egypt?

The sixth plague God sent upon Egypt was very similar to that which takes place in Revelation 16:2. The Bible describes the plague as "boils that break out in sores on man and beast throughout all the land of Egypt" (Exodus 9:9).

These sores may be a fulfillment of Old Testament prophecy. In Deuteronomy 28:27, 35, and Moses promised that God would judge Israel with boils and other skin diseases if they failed to walk in His covenant. The penalty for disobedience was that the plagues God visited upon Egypt (which included sores and boils [Exodus 9:9]) would be visited upon Israel.

The judgment mentioned in Revelation 16:10–11 is a plague of darkness. Once again, it is reminiscent of the plagues of Egypt. Just as the sores of the first plague are a symbol of the inner infection of those who bear them, this outer darkness is a reflection of the darkness of heart and soul of those who deny God.

[The Antichrist] will be the most powerful dictator the world has ever seen, making Caesar, Hitler, Mao, and Saddam seem weak and tame by comparison.

What is Armageddon?

Our nation is no stranger to war. In the less than 250 years of American history, we have been involved in nearly three hundred wars, conflicts, military operations.

The Bible tells us that there is yet another major war to be fought on this earth—sometime *after* the Russian-led coalition of nations' war against Israel. This war, called *Armageddon*, makes all the wars America has fought to date look like minor skirmishes. This war will draw the final curtain on modern civilization. In fact, preparations for that war are underway right now throughout the world. The only thing holding back its rapid approach is the yet-to-occur disappearance of all true believers in Jesus Christ, the event we know as the Rapture of the church. When the church of Jesus Christ is taken safely into heaven and the Tribulation period begins, the unrestrained satanic persecution of Israel will propel the entire world toward the Battle of Armageddon.

What does *Armageddon* mean?

Given the enormous attention this word receives, it may surprise you that Armageddon is mentioned only once in the Bible—in the sixteenth chapter of Revelation. The Hebrew word *harmageddon* means "the mount of Megiddo." *Har* means "mount," and *megiddo* means "slaughter"; so the meaning of *Armageddon* is "Mount of Slaughter."

Where will Armageddon take place?

Armageddon will take place on the mountain of Megiddo, located in northern Israel. It includes an extended plain that reaches from the Mediterranean Sea to the northern part of the land of Israel. Megiddo is about eighteen miles southeast of Haifa, fifty-five miles north of Jerusalem, and a little more than ten miles from Nazareth, the town where Jesus grew up.

While the word *Armageddon* is mentioned only once in the Bible, the mountain of Megiddo has a rich biblical history. It was at Megiddo that Deborah and Barak defeated the Canaanites (Judges 4 and 5). It was also there that Gideon defeated the Midianites (Judges 7); Saul was slain during a war with the Philistines (1 Samuel 31); Ahaziah was slain by Jehu (2 Kings 9); and Josiah was slain by the invading Egyptians (2 Kings 23).

These are not by any means the only battles that have been fought on this bloody ground. If we had stood on top of Megiddo over past centuries and overlooked the plain of Armageddon, we would have seen a long succession of waged battles as great armies marched across the field one after the other—the Crusaders, the Egyptians, the Persians, the Druze, the Greeks, the Turks, and the Arabs. During World War I, British general Edmund Allenby led his army against the Turks in a fierce battle on the Plain of Armageddon. According to scholar Alan Johnson, "More than 200 battles have been fought at or near there."[26] As you can see, Megiddo has earned its awful name: it is indeed a Mount of Slaughter.

Why will Megiddo be the location of the world's final conflict?

One of the world's greatest military figures gives us the answer. In 1799, Napoleon stood at Megiddo before the battle that ended his quest to conquer the East and rebuild the Roman Empire. Considering the enormous plain of Armageddon, he declared: "All the armies of the world could maneuver their forces on this vast plain . . . There is no place in the whole world more suited for war than this . . . [It is] the most natural battleground on the whole earth."[27]

While it is no mystery why the earth's final battle will be fought at Armageddon, it is important to understand that the battle will be centralized on that field but not contained there. All the ancient prophets agree that this war will be fought throughout the entire land of Israel.

The words of the prophet Zechariah describes Jerusalem as the center of conflict in the Armageddon war: "Behold, I will make Jerusalem a cup of drunkenness to all the surrounding peoples, when they lay siege against Judah and Jerusalem. And it shall happen in that day that I will make Jerusalem a very heavy stone for all peoples; all who would heave it away will surely be cut in pieces, though all nations of the earth are gathered against it" (Zechariah 12:2–3). So, while we use the term *Armageddon* and localize the war to the plain of Megiddo, Scripture teaches that the battle will literally fill the whole land of Israel with war and bloodshed.

What is the purpose of Armageddon in the plan of God?

1. To finish His judgment upon Israel: The Tribulation period is a time of divine indignation against the people of Israel, the people who rejected their Messiah and—time and time again after given the chance to return—failed to heed the corrective and punitive judgment of God. It is no accident that this future period of time is often referred to as "the time of Jacob's trouble" (Jeremiah 30:7).

2. To finalize His judgment upon the nations that have persecuted Israel: Those nations that have persecuted the Jewish people are finally gathered together in the Battle of Armageddon, in the Valley of Jehoshaphat, giving God the perfect opportunity to deal with them finally and decisively.

"I will also gather all nations, And bring them down to the Valley of Jehoshaphat; And I will enter into judgment with them there

On account of My people, My heritage Israel,
Whom they have scattered among the nations;
They have also divided up My land" (Joel 3:2).
3. To formally judge all the nations that have rejected
Him: "Now out of His mouth goes a sharp sword,
that with it He should strike the nations. And He
Himself will rule them with a rod of iron. He
Himself treads the winepress of the fierceness and
wrath of Almighty God" (Revelation 19:15).

Notice that last phrase: "He Himself treads the wine-press of the fierceness and wrath of Almighty God." To our time-bound senses God's activity often seems so slow and ponderous that people pursuing ungodly goals tend to dismiss His judgment as a factor to be taken seriously. Thus the nations do not believe that a time is coming when God's judgment will inevitably descend. But be assured, He is storing up judgment against a day to come. The Bible is clear: one of these days God will have had enough, and His judgment will pour down like consuming fire against the world's wicked nations.

> ## What is the difference between the Battle of Gog and the Battle of Armageddon?

At the beginning of the Tribulation period, Gog (the Prince of Russia/Magog) assembles a mass of nations against Israel that is thwarted by God's intervention. Armageddon will end the Tribulation period. The Battle of Gog and the Battle of Armageddon are separated by several years and involve different participants. Here are some of the differences that will help keep the two battles separate in your mind:

* In the Battle of Gog, Russia and at least five other nations are involved (Ezekiel 38:2–6). In the Battle of Armageddon, all the nations of the world are involved (Joel 3:2; Zechariah 14:2).
* In the Battle of Gog, the invaders will attack from the north (Ezekiel 38:6, 15; 39:2). In the Battle of Armageddon, the armies come from the north, south, east, and west (Daniel 11:40–45; Zechariah 14:2; Revelation 16:12–16).

- In the Battle of Gog, the purpose of the armies is to "take a spoil, and to take a prey" (Ezekiel 38:12 KJV). In the Battle of Armageddon, the purpose is to annihilate the Jews and to fight Christ and His army (Zechariah 12:2–3, 9; 14:2; Revelation 19:19).

- In the Battle of Gog, Russia will be the leader of the nations (Ezekiel 38:13). In the Battle of Armageddon, the Antichrist will be the leader (Revelation 19:19).

- In the Battle of Gog, God defeats the northern invaders with the convulsions of the earth, the confusion of the troops, the contagion of diseases, and calamities from the sky. In the Battle of Armageddon, the armies are defeated by the word of Christ—"a sharp sword" (Revelation 19:15, 21).

- In the Battle of Gog, Israel's enemies will perish upon the mountains of Israel and in the open field (Ezekiel 39:4–5). In the Battle of Armageddon, those slain by the Lord will lie where they fall, from one end of the earth to the other (Jeremiah 25:33).

- In the Battle of Gog, the dead will be buried (Ezekiel 39:12–15). In the Battle of Armageddon, the dead will not be buried, but their carcasses will be totally consumed by the birds (Jeremiah 25:33; Revelation 19:17–18, 21).

❖ After the battle of Gog, war will continue among the nations involved (other than Israel) during the remainder of the Tribulation (Revelation 13:4–7). After the Battle of Armageddon, swords and spears will be beaten into plowshares and pruning hooks (Isaiah 2:4). And the nations will study war no more.[28]

What will happen to the
Antichrist as he leads the
Battle of Armageddon?

During the Battle of Armageddon, the world will become increasingly discontented with the leadership of this global dictator who has gone back on every promise he made. Major segments of the world will begin to assemble their own military forces and rebel against him.

The king of the South and his armies will be the first to come after the Antichrist, followed by the armies of the North. "At the time of the end the king of the South shall attack him; and the king of the North shall come against him like a whirlwind, with chariots, horsemen, and with many ships" (Daniel 11:40).

The Antichrist will put down some of these first attempts at rebellion against him. But before he can celebrate and move on toward his goal of destroying Israel and Jerusalem, something happens: "But news from the east and the north shall trouble him; therefore he shall go out with great fury to destroy and annihilate many" (Daniel 11:44). The Bible leaves no doubt as to the source of the news that so disturbs and enrages the Antichrist: "Then the sixth angel poured out his bowl on the great river Euphrates, and its water was dried up, so that the way of the kings from the east might be prepared" (Revelation 16:12).

The Euphrates is one of the greatest rivers in the world. It flows from the mountains of western Turkey, through Syria, and continues on right through the heart of Iraq, not far from Baghdad. It eventually unites with the Tigris to become the *Shatt el Arab*, and finally empties into the Persian Gulf. The entirety of the Euphrates flows through Muslim territory. In Genesis 15 and Deuteronomy 11, the Lord specified that the Euphrates would be the easternmost border of the Promised Land. It serves both as a border and a barrier between Israel and her enemies.

What is the significance of the drying up of the Euphrates River, and why will that event have such a disturbing effect on the Antichrist?

Without water in the Euphrates River, there is no longer a barrier between the Antichrist and the vast army marching toward him. When this unprecedented army crosses the bed of the Euphrates against the Antichrist, the greatest war of all history involving hundreds of millions of people will be set in motion. The major battleground for that war will be the land of Israel.

As if this news is not frightening enough, John tells us that all these events are inspired and directed by the demons of hell: "For they are the spirits of demons, performing signs, which go out to the kings of the earth and of the whole world, to gather them to the battle of that great day of God Almighty" (Revelation 16:14).

No doubt demonism in every shape and form will manifest itself more and more as the end draws near, until at last it all ends in Armageddon . . . But besides these hosts of human armies, there will also be present at Armageddon an innumerable host of supernatural beings . . . So Armageddon will truly be a battle of heaven and earth and hell.[29]

So just at the moment when the Antichrist is about to attack and destroy Israel and Jerusalem, a diversion occurs in the form of another massive army entering the field of conflict. Thus the stage is set for the last, stunning movement in the Battle of Armageddon.

The Second Coming

To Judge the World

AFTER READING ABOUT THE RULE OF
THE ANTICHRIST, WE WILL FIND IT
REASSURING TO KNOW THAT CHRIST
WILL RETURN TO RULE AND REIGN OVER
THE EARTH AND TO JUDGE THE WORLD.

Christ's return will be amplified by a devastating spectacle that will make Hollywood disaster movies look like Saturday morning child's fare. The world will see and recognize its rightful Lord and King. Whereas He came the first time in humility and simplicity, this time His glory and majesty will be spectacularly displayed for all to see.

Will the earth be judged at the end of the Tribulation?

At the close of the Tribulation, Jesus Christ will come again to judge the earth. He will reconcile His chosen people to Himself, and the reign of the King of Kings will begin. Everlasting righteousness will be brought in during the Millennium. The Temple will be anointed and the beauty of Jewish worship reestablished in the millennial Temple.

❖ **Who is the Judge?**

Matthew 25:31–33 tells us clearly that the Son of Man is the Judge presiding over the judgment of nations. John 5:22 tells us that the Father will not judge anyone; He has committed all judgment to His Son, Jesus Christ. Not only that, but the Bible says that Jesus will come with His holy angels to pour out His judgment.

❖ **When is the Judgment?**

The time of this judgment is well established by premillennial students of the Scriptures. It takes place when the Son comes in all His glory, so this judgment will be at the Second Coming. This is not the Rapture when Christians will meet Christ in the air, but the Second Advent, when He will come to earth and end the Great Tribulation.

❖ **Where does the Judgment take place?**

This judgment will take place on earth, not in heaven. Jesus will have returned to sit on His glorious throne, and "of the increase of His government and peace there will be no end, upon the throne of David and over His kingdom, to order it and establish it with judgment and justice from that time forward, even forever. The zeal of the Lord of hosts will perform this" (Isaiah 9:7). Jesus Christ will reign over the restored earth for a thousand years (the Millennium) in His kingdom, then over a newly created heaven and earth for all eternity.

❖ **Who will be judged?**

The judgment will be over all the unbelievers on the earth (Revelation 19:15, 20, 21). At this time, Christ will return to earth with His raptured saints to judge the unsaved and reign over the earth. Though He will have taken the believers into heaven at the Rapture seven years earlier, others will have come to believe in Him during that dreadful time called the Tribulation. All those who have believed in Christ during the Tribulation will also reign with Him for a thousand years.

Exactly what does "Christ will reclaim the earth" mean?

The book of Revelation is divided into three sections. At the beginning of the book, we are introduced to the world ruined by man. As we move to the latter half of the Tribulation period, we witness the world ruled by Satan. But as we come to Christ's return at the end of the Tribulation period, we see the world reclaimed by Christ.

Reclaiming the earth, however, is not merely a simple matter of Christ's stepping in and planting His flag. Before the earth can be reclaimed, it must be cleansed. You wouldn't move back into a house infested with rats without first exterminating and cleaning it up. That is what Christ must do before He reclaims the earth. All rebellion must be rooted out. He must avenge the damage done to His perfect creation by wiping the rebels from the face of the earth.

How will the earth be cleansed?

Words are hardly adequate to describe the horror of this appalling scene. The fowls of the earth's air all gather at Armageddon to feast upon the massive piles of human flesh that will litter the battlefield for miles upon miles. The word translated *fowls* or *birds* is found only three times in the Bible: twice in Revelation 19 (vv. 17 and 21) and once more in Revelation 18:2. It is the Greek word *arnin*, which designates a scavenger bird that is best translated into the English as *vulture*.

In John's vision the angel is calling the vultures of the earth to Armageddon to "the supper of the Great God" where they will feast on the fallen carcasses of the enemies of the Lord. The text says that these corpses include both great and small, kings and generals, bond and free. As Harry Ironside says, "It is an awful picture—the climax of man's audacious resistance to God."[30]

> What is the comparison of references in the Bible regarding Christ's First and Second Advents?

Although Christians are most familiar with the first coming of Christ, it is the Second Coming that gets the most ink in the Bible. References to the Second Coming outnumber references to the first by a ratio of eight to one. Scholars count 1,845 biblical references to the Second Coming, including 318 in the New Testament. Christ's return is emphasized in no less than seventeen Old Testament books and seven out of every ten chapters in the New Testament. The Lord Himself refers to His return twenty-one times. The Second Coming is second only to faith as the most dominant subject in the New Testament.

Given the Old Testament prophecies of Christ's First and Second Advents, why did the Jews reject Him?

The Old Testament prophecies of Christ's First and Second Advents are so mingled that Jewish scholars did not clearly see them as separate events. Their perception of these prophecies was like viewing a mountain range from a distance. They saw what appeared to be one mountain, failing to see that there was another equally high mountain behind it, obscured from their sight through the perspective of distance. The prophets saw both comings of Christ either as one event or as very closely related in time. One Bible scholar has written: "Words spoken in one breath, and written in one sentence, may contain prophetic events millennia apart in their fulfillments."[31]

This mixing of two prophetic events into one may partially explain why the Jews as a whole have rejected Christ. The prophecies speak of the Messiah both enduring great suffering and accomplishing a great conquest. They thought the suffering Savior would become the conquering Savior in one advent. They did not realize He would come a first time to suffer and then a second time to conquer.

It is evident that even Jesus' followers expected Him to fulfill the glorious promises related to His second coming when He came the first time. Only after He ascended into heaven did they realize that they were living in the time period between His two appearances, as if on a plain between two mountains.

What will the Second Coming be like?

Matthew writes:

"For as the lightning comes from the east and flashes to the west, so also will the coming of the Son of Man be. For wherever the carcass is, there the eagles will be gathered together.

Immediately after the Tribulation of those days the sun will be darkened, and the moon will not give its light; the stars will fall from heaven, and the powers of the heavens will be shaken. Then the sign of the Son of Man will appear in heaven, and then all the tribes of the earth will mourn, and they will see the Son of Man coming on the clouds of heaven with power and great glory. And He will send His angels with a great sound of a trumpet, and they will gather together His elect from the four winds, from one end of heaven to the other" (Matthew 24:27–31).

The Second Coming will be a glorious event beheld by believers and unbelievers alike. It is a cataclysmic event that will usher in the Millennium, Christ's thousand year reign on earth (discussed in more detail later in these pages).

What are the differences between the Lord's first and second comings?

❖ In His first coming He was wrapped in swaddling clothes. In His second coming He will be clothed royally in a robe dipped in blood.

❖ In His first coming He was surrounded by cattle and common people. In His second coming He will be accompanied by the massive armies of heaven.

❖ In His first coming the door of the inn was closed to Him. In His second coming the door of the heavens will be opened to Him.

❖ In His first coming His voice was the tiny cry of a baby. In His second coming His voice will thunder as the sound of many waters.

❖ In His first coming He was the Lamb of God who came bringing salvation. In His second coming He will be the Lion of the tribe of Judah who comes bringing judgment.

Who will come with Christ at the Second Coming?

The great Lord Jesus, the Captain of the Lord's Hosts, the King over all Kings will descend to defend and protect His chosen people and put a once-and-for-all end to the evil of the Antichrist. But the Lord Jesus, Captain of the Lord's hosts, will not descend alone, as the following Scriptures make abundantly clear:

- ❖ "Thus the LORD my God will come, and all the saints with You" (Zechariah 14:5).
- ❖ " . . . the coming of our Lord Jesus Christ with all His saints" (1 Thessalonians 3:13).
- ❖ "when He comes, in that Day, to be glorified in His saints and to be admired among all those who believe . . ." (2 Thessalonians 1:10).
- ❖ "Behold, the Lord comes with ten thousands of His saints . . ." (Jude v. 14).

All those who have died in the Lord, along with those who were raptured before the years of the Tribulation,

Rapture / Second Coming Contrasts

Rapture / Translation	Second Coming Established Kingdom
1. Translation of all believers	1. No translation at all
2. Translated saints go to heaven	2. Translated saints return to earth
3. Earth not judged	3. Earth judged and righteousness established
4. Imminent, any moment, signless	4. Follows definite predicted signs, including tribulation
5. Not in the Old Testament	5. Predicted often in Old Testament
6. Believers only	6. Affects all humanity
7. Before the day of wrath	7. Concluding the day of wrath
8. No references to Satan	8. Satan bound
9. Christ comes *for* His own	9. Christ comes *with* His own
10. He comes in the *air*	10. He comes to the *earth*
11. He claims His bride	11. He comes with His bride
12. Only His own see Him	12. Every eye shall see Him
13. Tribulation begins	

Courtesy of Thomas Ice and Timothy Demy

will join with the Lord and participate in the battle to reclaim the world for the rule of Christ.

And the saints are not the only ones who will comprise the army of the Lord. Both Matthew and Paul tell us that the angels will also descend with Christ: "When the Son of Man comes in His glory, and all the holy angels with Him, then He will sit on the throne of His glory" (Matthew 25:31), "and when the Lord Jesus is revealed from heaven with His mighty angels" (2 Thessalonians 1:7).

How many angels are available for conscription into this army? The Bible shows their numbers to be staggering. In Matthew 26:52–53, Jesus told Peter in the Garden of Gethsemane, "Put your sword back in its place. . . Do you think that I cannot call on my father, and he will at once put at my disposal more than twelve legions of angels?" A Roman legion numbered about six thousand soldiers, so Jesus claimed instant access to the protection of 72,000 angelic soldiers who would have rushed to His rescue had He but said the word. Revelation 5:11 at the very least supports that number, saying, "I heard the voice of many angels around the throne, the living creatures, and the elders, and the number of them was ten thousand times ten thousand, and thousands of thousands." The Greek says literally,

". . . numbering myriads of myriads and thousands of thousands." The *New Living Translation* translates the passage as "thousands and millions of angels."

Christ will return not only to reward His own, but to judge the world. Between His first appearance and His second, will be a time of trouble, and then will occur the judgment of all those who rejected Him. This will not be a judgment for believers, for they have already stood before the Judgment Seat. This will be a judgment with no parole, no lenient sentence, and no pleas of insanity.

Escape the Coming Night

> When Christ returns at the Second Coming, will we know Him?

Because the Rapture takes place before the Second Coming, Christians will be in heaven with Christ during the Tribulation. At the time of the Second Coming, we will know Him because we will be with Him when He returns.

Revelation mentions the Supper of God and the Marriage Supper. Which will I attend?

There are two suppers mentioned in Revelation 19. The first is the Marriage Supper of the Lamb; the second is the Supper of God, in which the flesh of the foes of God is devoured by the scavenging birds. We are given our choice as to which supper we will attend. If we do not wish to eat the food at the Marriage Supper of the Lamb, we can become the food at the Supper of God. Christians will all be at the Marriage Supper of the Lamb—they will be the Bride of Christ!

What will happen to the Beast (Antichrist) and the False Prophet?

The Bible tells us that God simply snatches up the leader of the final rebellion—the Roman Antichrist—and flings him along with his co-conspirator, the False Prophet, into hell: "Then the beast was captured, and with him the false prophet who worked signs in his presence, by which he deceived those who received the mark of the beast and those who worshiped his image. These two were cast alive into the lake of fire burning with brimstone" (Revelation 19:20).

These two satanic creatures have the unwanted honor of actually getting to hell before Satan himself. As John tells us, Satan's confinement occurs much later: "The devil, who deceived them, was cast into the lake of fire and brimstone where the beast and false prophet are. And they will be tormented day and night forever and ever" (Revelation 20:10). Satan does not join the Beast and the False Prophet in hell until the end of the Millennium, one thousand years after their arrival.

What is the difference between the Judgment Seat of Christ and the Great White Throne Judgment?

At the beginning of the Tribulation, Christians will come before the Judgment Seat of Christ (2 Corinthians 5:10). After seven years and the Millennium (1,007 years later), there will be the Great White Throne Judgment—the judgment of God—when everyone will give an account.

No one can run away from the judgment of God. Revelation 20:13 states, "The sea gave up the dead who were in it, and Death and Hades delivered up the dead who were in them. And they were judged, each one according to his works." These dead, those who have rejected Christ, come before the Great White Throne Judgment. If their name is not found in the Book of Life, they are thrown into the lake of fire (Revelation 20:11–15).

**THE BELIEVERS' JUDGMENT
[THE JUDGMENT SEAT OF CHRIST]
IS AT THE BEGINNING OF THE TRIBULATION.**

**THEN THERE ARE SEVEN YEARS
[TRIBULATION]
AND THE MILLENNIUM.**

**AND THEN COMES THE
GREAT WHITE THRONE JUDGMENT.**

When are the hopeless souls
of the unredeemed thrown
into the Lake of Fire?

At the Great White Throne Judgment, every unre-deemed person who has ever lived will stand before Jesus Christ to receive the sentence of eternal death. There they will all face a Judge but no jury, a Prosecutor but no defender, a sentence but no appeal. It is the final judgment of the world. There is no hope for those who appear before the Great White Throne. There is no possibility of redemption, no possibility of a favorable verdict, and no possibility of appeal. There is only one sentence, and that is to be thrown into the lake of fire.

Is my name in the Book of Life?

The Book of Life is mentioned frequently in Scripture (Exodus 32–33; Psalm 69:28; Daniel 12:1 Philippians 4:3; Revelation 3:5; 13:8; 17:8; 21:27; 22:19), and it is imperative to make sure that your name is contained in it because that is your reservation for your eternal home with God. When you believe in Jesus Christ, you receive the free gift of eternal life and make your reservation in heaven. Those who do not receive God's free gift are blotted out. "Let them be blotted out of the book of the living, and not be written with the righteous" Psalm 69:28); "And anyone not found written in the Book of Life was cast into the lake of fire" (Revelation 20:15) where the souls of the damned will languish for all eternity. There, separated from the glory of God, they will remain in an unending state of hopeless agony.

The Millennium

To Rule the World

THE WORD *MILLENNIUM* IN LATIN
MEANS *MILLI* FOR "ONE THOUSAND"
AND *ANNUM* FOR "YEARS", WHICH
TRANSLATES TO "ONE THOUSAND
YEARS." DURING THAT TIME, CHRIST
WILL RULE ON EARTH IN PEACE AND
JUSTICE FROM THE CAPITAL IN
JERUSALEM. THE MILLENNIUM WILL
BE A FORETASTE OF THE HEAVENLY
STATE THAT IS TO FOLLOW.

Christ will come back when He is ready, and He will set up His kingdom without our help. That's why we need to be praying this great prayer with Isaiah: "Oh, that you would rend the heavens and come down" (Isaiah 64:1 NIV). We can say with John, "Amen. Even so, come, Lord Jesus" (Revelation 22:20). That's the only hope for lasting peace.

The Handwriting on the Wall

What is the meaning of the word *Millennium*?

*M*illennium* means "thousand years," and it refers to the period of time referred to in Revelation 20:1–6 which describes the rule and reign of Christ on earth. For a thousand years, Christ will rule as king over all the earth from His capital, Jerusalem. The saints of God, who returned with Him for the Battle of Armageddon, rule with Christ during the Millennium. We rule from the New Jerusalem and help to oversee a thousand years of peace and righteousness on earth. Satan will be bound during that period so that peace may flourish and the knowledge of the Lord may fill the earth. Everyone entering the Millennium will be a believer, having believed in Christ during the Tribulation.

The city is laid out as a cube in dimensions so enormous it defies the imagination. The length, width, and height of the cube are each said to measure twelve thousand furlongs or approximately 1,500 miles (Revelation 21:16). That makes a base alone of 2.25 million square miles! The ground floor alone would provide enough living space for far more people than have ever lived in the history of the world.

> ## Will Christ reign on earth for a literal one thousand years?

The duration of the Millennium is mentioned six times in Scripture and is never described in such a way as to suggest it should be taken symbolically or allegorically. The text is simple and straightforward: this earthly kingdom will last for one thousand years (Revelation 20:2–3).

What will the Millennium be like?

There will be no war. Kingdoms will be unified. Even the animal kingdom will be at peace (Micah 4:2–3; Isaiah 11:6–9). It will be a time of unrestrained prosperity. All want will be eliminated (Isaiah 35). Sin will be kept in check, and disobedience will be swiftly dealt with in this time of great purity. Christ's kingdom will be a holy kingdom (Isaiah 11:9, 66:23; Zechariah 13:2). During this time Satan will be bound and sealed so that he cannot go out to deceive the nations.

A man who dies at the age of one hundred will be thought accursed! There will be perpetual health. It appears that the extraordinary lifespan that characterized the race before the Flood will reappear (Isaiah 65:20). The Millennium will be an exhilarating era of happiness, contentment, and personal joy. It will be the answer to many ancient and anguished prayers (Isaiah 9:3–4; 12:3; 14:7–8; 25:8–9; 30:29; 42:1, 10–12).

What happens at the end of the Millennium?

During the Millennium, children will be born who will populate the earth. Some of these children will rebel against the righteous rule of God. Satan will be loosed for a time at the end of the Millennium as he stirs up a final rebellion on earth among those who haven't believed during the thousand years. The final judgment of the world, the Great White Throne Judgment, concludes the Millennium and ushers in the New Heaven and Earth (Revelation 20:11–15, 21:1).

What is the difference between Postmillennialism, Amillennialism, and Premillennialism?

These are three competing views concerning the Millennium.

❖ Postmillennialism teaches that the Church itself will bring about the Millennium through the preaching of the Gospel. As more and more people across the globe are converted, the world will gradually be conquered for Christ, and Jesus will at last return to earth to take up the throne won for Him by His Church.

❖ Amillennialism teaches that there is no literal one thousand-year reign of Christ. Instead, the Church inherits the millennial blessing promised to Israel, and Christ reigns through the Church right now in an allegorized millennium. This view was developed and promoted by Augustine in the fourth century and remains a common view in many Reformed circles.

❖ Premillennialism is the oldest view of the three and holds that Christ will physically return to earth to put down His enemies and reign over the earth for a literal one thousand-year period. This view is found in the writings of the earliest church Fathers and remains the most common view among evangelicals.

Because of the rule of a righteous King whose justice will keep life in balance around the world, many of the causes of heartache will be removed. The Millennium will be a time of unprecedented joy as a natural by-product of peace. Isaiah 14:7 says, "The whole earth is at rest and quiet; they break forth into singing."

What You Always Wanted to Know About Heaven

Why should one believe in a literal Millennium (Premillennialism)?

There are at least four reasons why Christ must come back to earth to reign personally over the kingdoms of the world.

❖ A literal Millennium is needed to reward the people of God. Scores of promises are scattered throughout both testaments guaranteeing that God's people will receive bountiful rewards for faithful service.

❖ A literal Millennium is needed to respond to the disciples' prayer recorded in Luke 11 and Matthew 6. When they prayed, "Your kingdom come," they were requesting that the long-awaited kingdom would be established.

❖ A literal Millennium is needed to redeem creation. Genesis 3 describes the horrors of a world cursed by God because of sin, while Romans 8:19–22 describes a coming time when that curse will be lifted. The Millennium is the only period in history where such a lifting of the curse can be found.

❖ A literal Millennium is needed to reemphasize man's depravity and the necessity of Christ's death on the cross. The Millennium will answer once and for all the age-old question of whether man's sin stems from environment or heritage. The Millennium will feature one thousand years of unbroken peace and prosperity, in which Christ will rule from Jerusalem with an iron rod. Yet at the end of that age of bliss, Satan will be loosed for a short time to demonstrate that the heart of man is indeed black with sin and that even in a perfect environment, unredeemed men will turn against God and rebel. The Millennium is proof positive that Christ's death is essential for mankind's salvation.

The New Heaven and the New Earth

To Create God's Eternal Kingdom

GOD HAS ESTABLISHED AN ETERNAL HOME FOR HIS CHILDREN WHERE THERE WILL BE NO SICKNESS OR DYING. FORMER SORROWS WILL NOT BE REMEMBERED AS HIS CHILDREN SPEND ETERNITY IN HIS PRESENCE, REJOICING IN THE NEW JERUSALEM.

✳

Can you imagine a holy city? It
will be a community where no
one lied, no shady business
deals were ever discussed, no
unclean movies or pictures were
seen. The New Jerusalem will be
holy because everyone in it will
be holy. Whatever discouraging
or dark thoughts enter our
minds today will be erased.

Escape the Coming Night

What will we do in heaven?

We will never grow bored! We will sing (Revelation 15:3–5). Those who could never carry a tune on earth will be able to sing in heaven and never grow weary of exalting the name of the King of Kings. We'll serve perfectly, enabled by the power that is able to conform all things to the pleasure of His sovereign will (Revelation 1:1; 7:3; 10:7; 11:18; 15:3; 19:5; 22:6). We'll share unbroken fellowship (Revelation 19:9, Hebrews 12:22–24) with angels, members of the Church, God, Jesus, and the spirits of just men made perfect. Never again will we have to say good-bye to a loved one or give a farewell party.

God has different things for different people to do. God made each of us unique with a special ministry and responsibility. Each of us in our own right has a purpose and design for what God has called us to do. There are many distinct groups in heaven, all unique in their responsibility before God. For instance, the twenty-four elders are crowned, enthroned, and seated (Revelation 4:10; 11:16). The 144,000 from the Tribulation have no crowns or thrones and are standing up and singing a song that no one else knows (Revelation 14:3). The song of the 144,000 sounds like great rushing waters and loud peals of thunder. It is joy filled (v. 14:2).

When we get to heaven, we are going to praise God in every conceivable way. All of heaven is filled with music. Worship music gives us a taste of heaven. There are more hymns in the book of Revelation than in any other book of the Bible, except for the book of Psalms. Music needs to be a high priority with us if we want to know how to worship the Lord.

Is there such a thing as "soul sleep"?

Revelation 6:9–11 strikes a deathblow to the idea of soul sleep. The souls under the altar who were martyred during the Tribulation are conscious and speaking: "And they cried with a loud voice, saying, 'How long, O Lord'"? We should not be led astray by the use of the word *sleep* in connection with the death of the body. This is not "soul sleep." We can understand more clearly when we read 1 Thessalonians 4:14–16. Here we are told about the resurrection of the believers: (1) they rise from the grave, and (2) God will bring them with Christ when He returns. There is only one way to explain how they can both rise and be brought from heaven. The soul and the body are separated in death. Sleep is applied only to the believer's body, which goes into the grave and awaits resurrection. Sleep is *never* applied to the soul of the believer.

Can anything keep the unsaved dead from hell?

No. That is why our primary goal is to reach as many people as possible before it is too late. There is no second chance, nor is there annihilation after death. At death the unsaved descend immediately into Hades where they are kept under punishment until their bodily resurrection—resulting in damnation (Daniel 12:2; Luke 16:22–24; Revelation 20:11–15).

As a Christian, why should I not fear death?

The Bible has a unique view of death for those who have placed their trust in Jesus Christ. It describes death for the believer as precious. "Precious in the sight of the Lord is the death of His saints" (Psalm 116:15). The Bible also describes death for the believer as being without sting. ("O death, where is your sting? O Hades, where is your victory?" [1 Corinthians 15:55]), and as being with Christ." ("For I am hard-pressed between the two, having a desire to depart and be with Christ, which is far better" [Philippians 1:23]). In heaven you will see Jesus face-to-face—"And God will wipe away every tear from their eyes; there shall be no more death, neither sorrow, nor crying, nor shall there be any more pain, for the former things have passed away" (Revelation 21:4 KJV). This is the wonderful hope with which we live!

Conclusion

THE SECOND COMING OF CHRIST IS
A CENTRAL THEME OF MUCH OF THE
BIBLE, AND IT IS ONE OF THE BEST-
ATTESTED PROMISES IN ALL OF
SCRIPTURE. CHRISTIANS CAN REST IN
THE SURE CONVICTION THAT JUST AS
JESUS CAME TO EARTH THE FIRST
TIME, SO HE WILL RETURN AT THE
CONCLUSION OF THE GREAT
TRIBULATION.

How should we prepare for the approaching End Times?

* *Stand Fast* (2 Thessalonians 2:15) This is not a time to go running after new doctrine. This is not the time to be exploring new ideas about theology. Stand fast in the truth that you know. If there has ever been a time for us to be unequivocal about our truth, this is it. The buzzword today is *tolerance*. But I want to be only as tolerant as God is, and God is quite intolerant of what is not true.

* *Hold On* (2 Thessalonians 2:15) The daily news can discourage us. But in the midst of it all, there is Jesus and His encouragement. We need to cultivate our relationship with Him until He is not just one of the things in our life, but He is the one thing in our life—the focus of who we are.

* *Work Hard* (2 Thessalonians 2:16–17; Luke 19:13 KJV) The objective of Christians is not only to go to heaven, but to take as many people with us as we can. Share the Gospel, teach children, build

one another up, strengthen one another, encourage those who are fallen, and reach out to those who are hurting. In every good work, "occupy till I come," said the Lord. This is no time for idleness. This is a time for us to seek the truth and live it out every day.

As we see the signs of the End
Times appearing, what shall
we do?

In spite of the high value I place on understanding future events, I find that studying prophecy has an even higher and more practical value. It provides a compelling motivation for living the Christian life. The immediacy of prophetic events shows the need to live each moment in Christlike readiness. When we have heard and understood the truth of Christ's promised return, we cannot just keep living our lives in the same old way. Future events have present implications that we cannot ignore. When we know that Christ is coming again to this earth, we cannot go on being the same people.

From the New Testament epistles, I have gleaned ten ways in which we should be different as a result of our prophetic knowledge. In each Scripture quotation, I have italicized the words connecting the admonition with the promise of Christ's return.

1. **Refrain from judging others**: "Therefore judge nothing before the time, *until the Lord comes*, who will both bring to light the hidden things of darkness and reveal the counsels of the hearts. Then each one's praise will come from God" (1 Corinthians 4:5).

2. **Remember the Lord's Table**: "For as often as you eat this bread and drink this cup, you proclaim the Lord's death *till He comes*" (1 Corinthians 11:26).

3. **Respond to life spiritually**: "If then you were raised with Christ, seek those things which are above, where Christ is, sitting at the right hand of God. Set your mind on things above, not on things on the earth. For you died, and your life is hidden with Christ in God. *When Christ who is our life appears*, then you also will appear with Him in glory" (Colossians 3:1–4).

4. **Relate to one another in love**: "And may the Lord make you increase and abound in love to one another and to all, just as we do to you, so that He may establish your hearts blameless in holiness before our God and Father at *the coming of our Lord Jesus Christ* with all His saints" (1Thessalonians 3:12–13 ; Jude v. 21).

5. **Restore the bereaved**: "But I do not want you to be ignorant, brethren, concerning those who have fallen asleep, lest you sorrow as others who have no hope. For if we believe that Jesus died and rose again, even so God will bring with Him those who sleep in Jesus.

   For this we say to you by the word of the Lord, that we who are alive and remain *until the coming of the Lord* will by no means precede those who are asleep. For the Lord Himself will descend from heaven with a shout, with the voice of an archangel, and with the trumpet of God. And the dead in Christ will rise first. Then we who are alive and remain shall be caught up together with them in the clouds to meet the Lord in the air. And thus we shall always be with the Lord. Therefore comfort one another with these words" (1 Thessalonians 4:13–18).

6. **Recommit ourselves to the ministry**: "I charge you therefore before God and the Lord Jesus Christ, who will judge the living and the dead *at His appearing* and His kingdom: Preach the word! Be ready in season and out of season. Convince, rebuke, exhort, with all longsuffering and teaching" (2 Timothy 4:1–2).

7. **Refuse to neglect church**: "And let us consider one another in order to stir up love and good works, not forsaking the assembling of ourselves together, as is the manner of some, but exhorting one another, and so much the more *as you see the Day approaching*" (Hebrews 10:24–25).

8. **Remain steadfast**: "Therefore be patient, brethren, until the coming of the Lord. See how the farmer waits for the precious fruit of the earth, waiting patiently for it until it receives the early and latter rain. You also be patient. Establish your hearts, for *the coming of the Lord is at hand*" (James 5:7–8).

9. **Renounce sin in our lives**: "And now, little children, abide in Him, that *when He appears*, we may have confidence and not be ashamed before Him *at His coming*. If you know that He is righteous, you know that everyone who practices righteousness is born of Him" (1 John 2:28–29).

10. **Reach the lost**: "Keep yourselves in the love of God, *looking for the mercy of our Lord Jesus Christ* unto eternal life. And on some have compassion, making a distinction; but others save with fear, pulling them out of the fire, hating even the garment defiled by the flesh" (Jude 21–23).

Why should I study prophecy and the book of Revelation?

S uch a careful writer as John is not likely to leave us wondering how we ought to apply the message of Revelation. He makes his purposes for writing the book crystal clear. You can be blessed just by reading the book (Revelation 1:3, 22:7) or cursed for tampering with it (vv. 22:18–19). The road to true success, Revelation tells us, is found in submitting our lives to God's Word. Revelation teaches us that although someday the need for evangelism will disappear, the need and privilege of worship is eternal. Practice "down here" before we worship Him perfectly "up there"!

We are under the same instruction that John received to take the words of the Gospel to men, women, boys and girls who do not yet know and love the Savior. "We must all appear before the judgment seat of Christ, that each one may receive the things done in the body, according to what he has done, whether good or bad" (2 Corinthians 5:10).

We must make ourselves ready now and watch for His coming because we have received ample warning

that He is coming and that there will be no time to prepare: "Surely I am coming quickly" (Revelation 22:20).

Now we reach the end of our
journey and will be given a
preview of eternity future; a
new heaven and a new earth
will be created. Although it is
difficult to imagine anything
more wonderful than the
heaven we inhabit upon our
deaths, the eternal heaven will
be even more glorious. The
crowning jewel in paradise will
be the holy city, the New
Jerusalem.

Escape the Coming Night

Endnotes

1. David McCullough, *Truman* (New York: A Touchstone Book published by Simon & Schuster, 1992), 619.

2. The Jewish People Policy Planning Institute: Annual Assessment 2007. (Jerusalem, Israel: Gefen Publishing House LDT, 2007), 15.

3. Robert J. Morgan, *My All in All* (Nashville, TN: B&H Publishing, 2008), entry for April 22.

4. Paul Crespo. "Something Is Going On Between Russia and Iran". 1/30/07. http://archive.newsmax.com/archives/articles/2007/1/29/212432.shtml?s=1h.

5. Joel C. Rosenberg, *Epicenter* (Carol Stream, IL: Tyndale, 2005), 113.

6. John Walvoord and Mark Hitchcock, *Armageddon, Oil and Terror* (Carol Stream, IL; Tyndale House Publishers, 2007), 67.

7. "Transatlantic Economic Council." http://ec.europa.eu/enterprise/enterprise_policy/inter_rel/tec/index_en.htm. Accessed 3/28/08.

8. Jerome R. Cossi. "Premeditated Merger: Inside the hush-hush North American Union confab." 3/13/08. www.worldnetdaily.com/index.php?pageId=39523.

9. Arno Froese, *How Democracy Will Elect the Antichrist* (Columbia, SC: The Olive Press, 1997), 165.

10. www.whitehouse.gov/news/release/2002/01/print/20030239-11html.

11. Scott Peterson. "Russia, Iran Harden Against West." *The Christian Science Monitor.* www.csmonitor.com 10/18/07.

12. AFP: "Russia scraps Libya's debts as Putin visits Tripoli." www.google.com/article/ALeqM5AgDZCvyaEv18qMczqwwc1-Er_w. 4/17/08.

13. Matthew Kreiger. "7,200 Israeli millionaires today, up 13%." *Jerusalem Post,* 6/28/07.

14. www.prosperity.org/profile.aspx?is+IS.

15. Statistics compiled from www.adherents.com/Religions_By_Adherents.html and http://pewresearch.org/assets/pdf/muslim-american.pdf. Download, page 15.

16. Quoted on authority of Ibn 'Abbas in Sahih of al-Bukhari; attested by numerous Islamic scholars. See, for example, http://www.bibletopics. com/BIBLESTUDY/96a.htm and http: www.giveshare. org/islam/index. html.

17. Information on the history of Islam is from Winfried Corduan, *Pocket Guide to World Religions* (Downers Grove: InterVarsity Press, 2006), 80–85.

18. Benazir Bhutto, *Reconciliation: Islam, Demoncray, and the West.* (New York: Harper Collins, 2008), 2,3,20.

19. Georges Sada, *Saddam's Secrets: How an Iraqi General Defied and Survived Saddam Hussein,* (Brentwood, TN: Integrity Publishers, 2006), 286–287.

20. "Vatican: Muslims now outnumber Catholics." *USAToday* 3/30/08. www.usatoday.com.

21. "Ahmadinejad's 2005 address to the United Nations" by Mahmoud Ahmadinejad. Translation provided by the United Nations.

22. "Ahmadinejad: Wipe Israel off map." http://english. aljazeera.net/English/archive/archive?ArchiveId=15816

23. Stan Goodenough, "Ahmadinejad:Israel has reached its 'final'stage.'" www.jnewswire.com/article/2314. 1/30/08

24. Mark Bentley and Ladane Nasseri, "Ahmadinejad's Nuclear Mandate Strengthened After Iran Election." www.bloomberg.com/ apps/news?pid=20601087&sid=aGUPH1VLn.7c&refer=home.

25. www.merriam-webster.com/dictionary/rapture.

26. Alan Johnson, *The Expositor's Bible Commentary* vol. 12 (Grand Rapids: Zondervan, 1981), 551.

27. Vernon J. McGee, T*hrough the Bible* vol. 3 (TN: Nashville, Thomas Nelson Publishers, 1982), 513.

28. From J. Dwight Pentecost, *Things to Come: A Study in Biblical Eschatology*(Findlay, OH: Dunham Publishing Company, 1958), 347, 348.

29. *The Coming Great War: The Greatest Ever Known in Human History* (Toronto, Canada: A. Sims, Publisher, 1932), 12–13.

30. H. A. Ironside, *Revelation*, (Grand Rapids, MI: Kregel reprint, 2004), 189.

31. Lehman Strauss, "Bible Prophecy": www.bible.org. Accessed 11/27/07.

If you enjoyed this book, you might want to consider these other works by Dr. Jeremiah.

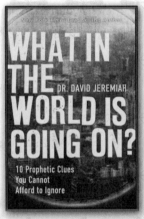

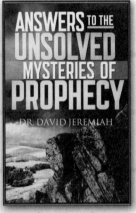

Ten straightforward, easy to understand scriptural prophecies are laid out as a guideline for sorting out *What in the World Is Going On?*

A booklet available through *Turning Point Ministries*

P.O. Box 3838,
San Diego, CA 92163

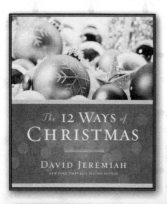

Twelve truths of Christmas—like wonder, giving, humility, and simplicity—that often get buried under the busyness of the season, are presented with candor and wisdom.

1 Minute a Day is a quick shot of espresso for your soul, with 100 one-minute reminders of what's really important.

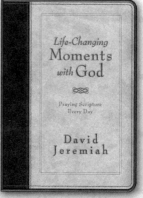

A 365-Day Devotional featuring Dr. Jeremiah's favorite selections from the *Daily Light* paraphrased as Scripture-based prayers.